RV OWNERS OPERATION & MAINTENANCE MANUAL

2nd EDITION

Published by

INTERTEC PUBLISHING CORPORATION
P.O. Box 12901, Overland Park, Kansas 66282-2901

The publisher has exercised reasonable care in compiling the information contained in this manual. The publisher does not guarantee the applications set forth in this manual to the extent that the operation of the equipment and its accessories may be subject to outside influences or factors which cannot be reasonably foreseen. The publisher shall in no way be liable for damages of any description to persons or property, whether incidental or consequential or otherwise related to the use of this manual and in no event shall the liability of the publisher exceed the price paid for this manual.

The RV Owners Operation & Maintenance Manual is provided to assist you in obtaining general information concerning the proper use and maintenance of your unit. It is not designed for one specific model. All RV manufacturers maintain the policy of continual design and manufacturing improvements, which requires that models, specifications and equipment be subject to change without notice. It is for this reason we wish to point out that in the event of conflicting instructions, illustrations or other descriptions, the information furnished by the respective component manufacturer's publications should be followed.

CONTENTS

(By Starting Page Number)

CONTENTS Continued

CONTENTS Continued

CONTENTS Continued

PREFACE

This **RV Owners Operation & Maintenance Manual** is an introduction to the world of recreational camping...and more specifically, **your camping vehicle.** We've included a variety of information for veteran as well as first-time campers, so that all of your trips (including the first) will be enjoyable experiences.

Most of the information in this manual will be useful to all campers, but special sections are included that describe operation and maintenance unique to specific types. As an example, instructions for hitching a trailer will only be important if you are pulling a trailer.

A primary goal of this publication is to impress the importance of always thinking and practicing safety when traveling and camping. Much of the information you'll find here is concerned with safe operation, but we can only convey safety information if you read this manual thoroughly. The operator is ultimately responsible for the safety of his passengers...his vehicle...and himself.

We hope you'll find this manual an important reference tool as you begin camping, but also hope that it remains a valuable reference source after many long successful trips.

We wish you many safe years of enjoyment with your RV.

The Editors
Technical Publications

INTRODUCTION

Your recreational vehicle has been designed and engineered to provide you with many self-contained comforts of home without having to be connected to outside sources. When parking where service facilities are available, external connections allow easy hook-up to water, electricity and waste disposal.

This manual was prepared to assist you in understanding the proper use and operation of various containment systems, maintenance of component parts and explanation of your warranty protection. If you are a newcomer to RV travel, you will especially appreciate the many tips, suggestions and "shop talk" information to be found throughout this manual which can help you learn how to obtain the most pleasure from the use of your vehicle.

Your RV has been provided with quality time-tested materials and components and if operated within recommended procedures, should provide you with many miles of virtually trouble-free travel. After the initial running-in period and usual minor adjustments to components and systems, only simple routine servicing is thereafter required.

We have made every effort to make this manual as accurate as possible in order to reflect information available at time of publication. Products are constantly being improved and manufacturers upgrade their installations accordingly. In event of conflicting instructions, illustrations or other descriptions, the information furnished by the respective manufacturer's separate publications should be followed.

The RVIA seal affixed to your RV certifies that your vehicle complies with applicable requirements of Federal Motor Vehicle Safety Standards, State Regulations, and complies with requirements of ANSI Standard A119.2 and National Electrical Code ANSI/NFPA 70, the nationally recognized "Standard for Recreational Vehicles-Installation of Plumbing, Heating and Electrical Systems."

TAKING DELIVERY

INSPECTION. Your RV is a product which has undergone a series of rigid inspections by highly qualified factory personnel throughout the manufacturing process. Final factory checks by quality control inspectors before shipment to the dealer is not the last one before you take delivery. Your dealer has been factory trained to perform additional pre-delivery inspections and system checks, condition and service your RV if necessary. He will also assist you in understanding operation, owner maintenance and dealer service policies. You may also need the dealer's help in understanding and completing warranty forms. It is important that you become familiar with the proper procedures for obtaining service and parts, in and out of warranty. Your dealer can provide you with this information at time of delivery.

MOTORHOME

Make: Model: Type _____

_____

Floor Plan* _____

Length _____ Year _____

Chassis Make _____

Chassis Model _____

Vehicle Identification Number _____

Internal Tracking Number _____

Purchase Date (month, day, year) _____

License Number _____ Club Number _____

Gross Vehicle Weight Rating (GVWR) —

    Front Axle _____ lbs. Rear Axle _____ lbs.

    Total _____ lbs.

Tires - Size _____ _____

    Identification Numbers _____

_____

Major Additions or Up-Grades _____

_____

*See abbreviations on following page.

TRAILER

Make: Model: Type: _____

Floor Plan* _____

Length _____ Year _____

Vehicle Identification Number _____

Purchase Date (month, day, year) _____

License Number _____ Club Number _____

Gross Vehicle Weight Rating (GVWR) —

    Each Axle (GAWR) _____ lbs.

    Hitch Weight Limit _____ lbs.

    Total Weight _____ lbs.

Tire Size _____

Identification Numbers _____

_____

Major Additions or Up-Grades _____

_____

_____

*See abbreviations below.

FLOOR PLANS —

A manufacturer may have several models with the same length; the difference being floor plan of interior layout. Abbreviations for most floor plans are included below as an aid in identifying the specific model.

BH	Bunkhouse	RD	Rear Dinette
CB	Center Bath	RK	Rear King
CC	Captain Chairs	RLR	Rear Living Room
CD	Center Dinette	RL	Rear Lounge
CK	Center Kitchen	RS	Rear Shower
D	Dinette	RT	Rear Twin
DB	Double Bed or	S	Sofa
	Double Bunk	SB	Side Bath or Split
FK	Front Kitchen		Bath
FL	Front Lounge	SD	Side Dinette
FS	Front Sofa	SK	Split Kitchen
KB	King Bed	SL	Side Lounge
LK	Long Kitchen	SLR	Side Living Room
MB	Master Bedroom	SS	Side Sofa
QB	Queen Bed	TB	Twin Bed
RB	Rear Bath or	WTB	Walk Through
	Rear Bedroom		Bedroom

DEALER

Company Name _____

Street Address _____

City, State & Zip Code _____

Telephone Number _____/ _____- _____

Sales Person _____

Service Person _____

MANUFACTURER

Company Name _____

Street Address _____

City, State & Zip Code _____

Customer Relation Phone
    Number _____/ _____- _____

_____

_____

CHECK LISTS

A check list can be a valuable aid for both you and your dealer as you prepare to take delivery of your RV. The check list on the following pages includes most of the items which should be checked and also provides space to write explanations. The dealer's representative will often suggest maintenance intervals, cleaning procedures and other helpful hints during your delivery inspection.

EXTERIOR CHECK LIST

	Condition Accepted	Operation Understood	Additional Comments
FRONT			
Skin			
Window(s)/Screens(s)			
Lights & Lens (Headlights, Park, Clearance, Turn, Etc.)			
Rock Shield			
Bumper			
Trailer Torque & Coupling .			
Tongue Jack(s) & Wheel(s) .			
Other			
LEFT SIDE			
Skin			
Window(s)/Screen(s)			
Entry Door & Lock			
Lights & Lens (Door & Clearance)			
Tires: Wheels and Hubcaps Front - Pressure			
Rear - Pressure			
Wheel Bearing — Lube & Serv. Interval . .			
Other			
REAR			
Skin			
Window(s)/Screen(s)			
Entry Door & Lock			
Lights & Lens (Stop, Tail, Turn, Clearance, License, etc.)			
Bumper			
Spare Tire & Wheel (Pressure)			
Trailer Hitch			
Other			

	Condition Accepted	Operation Understood	Additional Comments
RIGHT SIDE			
Skin			
Window(s)/Screen(s)			
Awning			
Entry Door(s) & Lock(s)			
Lights & Lens (Door & Clearance)			
Tires: Wheels and Hubcaps			
Front - Pressure			
Rear - Pressure			
Wheel Bearing — Lube & Serv. Interval ..			
Other			
ROOF			
Skin			
Vents			
Air Conditioner			
TV/Radio Antennae			
Other			
POTABLE WATER SUPPLY			
Storage Tank(s)			
Capacity			
Filling Equip. & Method ...			
Fill Date			
Plumbing (for leaks)			
Other			
GRAY WATER SYSTEM			
Plumbing (for leaks)			
Holding Tanks			
Drain Equip. & Method			
Other			

EXTERIOR CHECK LIST Cont.

	Condition Accepted	Operation Understood	Additional Comments
SEWER SYSTEM			
Plumbing (for leaks)			
Holding Tank(s)			
Hose & Adapter			
Drain Equip. & Method			
Other			
MISC.			
Canvas			
Entry Step(s)			
Electric Cord			
Stabilizers			
Leveling Jacks			
Vehicle Jack: Location & Operation			
Compartment Door(s) & Lock(s)			
Battery			
LP Gas Bottles, Regulator & Hose			
Filled Date			
Generator Set			
Service Intervals			
Furnace			
Storage Compartments			
Other			

INTERIOR CHECK LIST

DOORS, WINDOWS, WALLS, ETC.	Condition Accepted	Operation Understood	Additional Comments
LIVING ROOM/LOUNGE			
Door(s), Screen(s) & Lock(s)			
Window(s) & Screen(s) .			
Walls**			
Ceiling**			
Floor**			
Carpet/Flooring***			
Other			
KITCHEN/DINETTE			
Door(s), Screen(s) & Lock(s)			
Window(s) & Screen(s) .			
Walls**			
Ceiling**			
Floor**			
Carpet/Flooring***			
Other			
SLEEPING/BEDROOM			
Door(s), Screen(s) & Lock(s)			
Window(s) & Screen(s) .			
Walls**			
Ceiling**			
Floor**			
Carpet/Flooring***			
Other			
BATH ROOM			
Door, Screen & Lock ...			
Window(s) & Screen(s) .			
Walls**			
Ceiling**			
Floor**			
Carpet/Flooring***			
Other			

**Check for damage including: Scratches, Cracks, Bulges, Breaks, Separation or Water Damage.

***Check condition and note any special cleaning instructions.

	Condition Accepted	Operation Understood	Additional Comments
ELECTRICAL SERVICE			
Circuit Breakers			
Generator Set			
Converter			
Living Room/Lounge —			
Lights & Lamps			
Wall Plugs			
Power Vents or Fans . . .			
Kitchen/Dinette —			
Lights & Lamps			
Wall Plugs			
Power Vent(s)			
Sleeping/Bedroom —			
Lights & Lamps			
Wall Plugs			
Bathroom —			
Lights			
Wall Plugs			
Power Vent			
APPLIANCES			
REFRIGERATOR —			
12V(DC), 110V(AC), LP Gas			
Shelves, Trays, Doors . .			
Ice Maker			
RANGE & OVEN —			
Burners, Grilles, Racks			
Controls & Covers			
Vent & Filter			
MICROWAVE —			
Racks & Doors			
Controls & Accessories			
WASHER & DRYER			
BLENDER			

INTERIOR CHECK LIST Cont.

FURNISHINGS	Condition Accepted	Operation Understood	Additional Comments
LIVING ROOM/LOUNGE			
Cabinets			
Tables			
Curtains/ Drapes/Blinds***			
Furniture			
TV/Stereo/Radio(s)			
KITCHEN/DINETTE			
Cabinets			
Tables/Counters			
Curtains/Drapes/Blinds .			
Furniture			
Other			
SLEEPING/BEDROOM			
Cabinets			
Tables			
Curtains/ Drapes/Blinds***			
Bed(s)			
Other			
BATH ROOM			
Cabinets			
Counter			
Curtains/ Drapes/Blinds***			
Bath/Shower			
Other			

***Check condition and note any special cleaning instructions.

WATER SUPPLY			
Water Pump			
Switch Location			
Fuse Location & Size . . .			
Water Heater			
Kitchen Sink			
Lavatory			
Tub/Shower			

INTERIOR CHECK LIST Cont.

	Condition Accepted	Operation Understood	Additional Comments
Water Supply Cont.			
Pressurized Plumbing (For Leaks)			
Kitchen Sink			
Lavatory			
Tub/Shower			
GRAY-WATER SYSTEM			
Kitchen Sink			
Tub/Shower			
Lavatory			
Plumbing (For Leaks)			
SEWER SYSTEM			
Toilet.................			
Plumbing (For Leaks)			
AIR CONDITIONER			
Filter & Controls + ...			
Loose or Missing Parts ...			
Lube/Clean/Service Intervals			
FURNACE			
Pilot Light..............			
Filter & Control + ...			
Loose or Missing Parts ..			
Cleaning/Serv. Intervals ..			

+ Check operation, condition and note any special cleaning instructions.

SAFETY			
Smoke Detectors + + ...			
Fire Extinguishers			
Note Locations + + ...			
Leak Detectors (LP Gas) .			
Emergency Exits + + ...			

+ + Check location and operation.

YOUR DEALER. Selecting a dealership can be just as important as selecting the right RV. If you intend to buy from a dealer, evaluate the dealership as well as the RV's. If you don't buy from a dealer, first check out the dealers who service and stock parts for your rig. In some localities, it might require some extra mileage to find the good dealer who will work with you, but it will be worth it if you must depend heavily on a dealer.

When evaluating a dealership, consider the following points:

1. Is the dealership clean and well-organized?

2. Are the personnel courteous and are the sales-people, service department people and parts department people knowledgeable?

3. Are the service and parts department areas clean, well-organized and efficient?

4. Are the service and parts department hours convenient for you?

5. Ask the dealership for recent customer references and ask the Better Business Bureau for comments.

Try to build a good business relationship with the dealership personnel. Note the word BUSINESS here. They are there to make a living just like everyone else. Don't monopolize their time with unnecessary chitchat when there are other customers waiting. When you enter the dealership for parts or service, know as much about the part you need or the problem you are having as you possibly can. Insufficient information can make the job more difficult for the partsman or mechanic and may force you to travel home for the needed information.

Be just as friendly to the dealership personnel as you expect them to be to you. This friendly attitude may result in some special help in the future.

A good recreational vehicle dealer is helpful in many ways, including the following:

☐ Providing the customer with an adequate orientation in the general operation of the RV, use of its containment systems and components and safety considerations concerning the use of those systems.

☐ Ensuring that the customer receives a complete owners packet containing warranty cards and various registrations for the RV and separately warranted products and accompanying literature, including all operating, installation and maintenance instructions as required.

☐ Reviewing all warranty entitlements with the customer, pointing out the importance of mailing warranty cards and registrations to various manufacturers within ten (10) days of taking delivery. The dealer will often assist the customer in properly completing these forms if he desires. It is important that the customer read all warranty information as soon as possible and contact the dealer to clear up any provisions which are not understood.

☐ Performing all of the prescribed pre-delivery inspections. The check lists included in this book may be helpful for both the dealer and the owner while inspecting the RV. Items included are to remind both parties of things to check. Operation and regular maintenance to such items as the refrigerator, furnace, generator set, etc., should be explained by the dealer. The owner should then mark in the appropriate area that he understands the proper operation.

☐ The dealer can assist the customer concerning insurance considerations for his protection.

☐ Many dealers can help the owner find approved service, both locally and while traveling. Separate systems installed in the RV are often warrantied and serviced by companies specializing in repair of product. Knowing where to obtain proper maintenance while traveling can be especially valuable to the owner.

INSURANCE. As with your automobile, it is important that you protect yourself and others with insurance coverages for personal liability, theft, collision, overturn, property damage, etc. Your dealer will assist you in obtaining appropriate insurance for your protection.

There are numerous reliable insurance companies that specialize in providing insurance for recreational vehicles. It may pay you to check with the company that now provides your automobile or pick-up truck insurance. Many times adequate recreational vehicle insurance may also be obtained as a rider to your automobile or truck policy at considerable savings. Don't put off insuring yourself for RV coverage.

CANADIAN AND MEXICAN. Insurance for travel in Canada can usually be covered by your present U.S. Policy for the recreational vehicle, often at no extra cost. Consult your individual insurance company for procedures and be sure of your coverage before entering Canada.

For travel in Mexico, it is recommended that you buy Mexican insurance at the border. Although your U.S. policy might cover you, if you are involved in an accident in Mexico and do not have a Mexican policy, the investigative delays can be quite lengthy. Always consult your U.S. insurance company when planning a trip into Mexico.

It is also suggested that all items should be engraved with an identification mark to assist recovery. Many service organizations provide free use of equipment for marking personal property. Check with local law enforcement agencies for suggested method of marking and for availability of marking equipment. The cost of an electric vibrator engraving tool is very little and it is convenient to have available for marking new equipment.

List personal property located in the RV using the form on page 22 or similar form available from most insurance agents. Store this list in a safety deposit or similar location away from the RV. This record will be a valuable help if items are lost, stolen or destroyed.

INVENTORY OF PERSONAL PROPERTY
LOCATED IN RV
(Store this record in a Safe place away from RV)

Item	Serial No.	Value

INSURANCE

Company _____

Policy No. _____

Agent's Name _____

Address _____

Business Phone _____

Home Phone _____

Emergency Phone _____

WARRANTIES

WARRANTY EXPLANATION. The RV warranty is designed to cover defects in material and workmanship on the RV unit. This warranty is provided by the RV manufacturer and most warranty problems are handled at the dealer level. Since the RV warranties vary from manufacturer to manufacturer, it is important that warranty on the unit be carefully read and discussed with the dealer when taking delivery.

Normally, this warranty does not extend to damage from neglect, accidents, misuse, or failure to follow service and use instructions, lack of proper maintenance, normal fair wear and tear, unauthorized repairs or unauthorized modifications to any part of containment systems or body that might cause defective performance. The manufacturer does not assume the responsibility for loss of use of vehicle, loss of time, inconvenience or expenses due to equipment failure.

SEPARATELY WARRANTED PRODUCTS. The RV manufacturer assumes no responsibility or liability for defects in the workmanship or operation of separately warranted products. These products are warranted by the individual manufacturers and a copy of their warranty, if available, has been included in your owners packet. In order to obtain repairs or replacement of these items, the individual manufacturers warranty cards must be submitted within ten (10) days of date of purchase.

If service or parts are required for these products, refer to the furnished list of factory authorized service centers. If the list is not available for the particular products, write or call the manufacturer concerned to obtain the location of the nearest authorized service center.

SAFETY

SAFETY IN USING LP-GAS. You should check for leaks at the connections on the LP-Gas system soon after purchase and initial filling of LP tanks, and continued periodic checks of the system are recommended. Even though the manufacturer and dealer have already checked for leaks, you should also check regularly, because the vibration encountered during travel can loosen connections or cause cracks. Your vehicle was manufactured to provide you with full access to all gas line connections. Leaks can be found easily with a soapy water solution applied to the outside of the gas piping connections. Usually tightening the connections will stop leaks. If not, ask your authorized dealer service to make the necessary repairs.

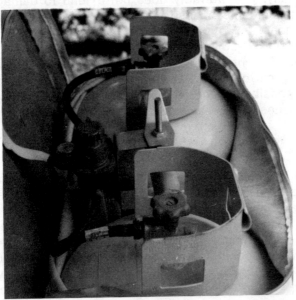

LP-Gas is heavier than air. Leaking gas tends to flow to low places, much as will water. It will sometimes pocket in a low area. LP-Gas can usually be detected by an identifiable odor similar to onions or garlic. Never light a match or allow any open flame in the presence of leaking gas.

Be sure to shut off the main LP-Gas supply valve while refueling the vehicle to prevent any accidental ignition of gasoline fumes by the pilot lights in the water heater, furnace or refrigerator.

Never allow gas tanks to be filled above the liquid capacity indicated on the tank. If a tank is overfilled, liquid gas may flow through the regulator causing it to freeze and/or introduce a dangerous excessive gas pressure into the lines. In addition, an overfilled tank placed in hot sunlight may expel excess gas through the relief valve and be susceptible to ignition by any nearby open flame.

ELECTRICAL SYSTEM SAFETY. As delivered, your RV has been engineered and checked for your complete safety. Circuit breakers and fuses are installed to protect electrical circuits from overloading. Do not make unauthorized changes to circuitry or add on fixed appliances yourself. If you wish to make changes, consult your dealer and he will assist you in obtaining a safe installation.

An approved power supply cord has been supplied with the vehicle. Always use this cord for hook-up to the 120 volt source. Note that the cord has a three pin plug which provides proper grounding through the third (round) pin. Grounding is your personal protection from electrical shock. Do not use any adapter, cheater or extension cord that will break the continuity of the grounding circuit connected to that third pin.

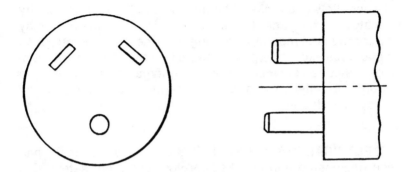

View of the approved 120 volt 3-pin plug used on power supply cords. Safety grounding is through the third (round pin).

NEVER remove the grounding pin for convenience of being able to connect to a non-grounded (2-prong) receptacle. Use a grounding adapter with two prongs plus a **"pig-tail" conductor which should be externally grounded.**

NEVER operate your RV with a "hot skin". If you can feel even a small shock from the RV while standing on the ground, you should immediately disconnect the RV from power source and locate the trouble. The fault is usually from a break in the grounding circuit which should be continuous from the skin or frame to the distribution panel board to the third pin on the power supply cord and then back to the park receptacle and earth ground.

EMERGENCY STOPPING SAFETY. Always carry road flares and/or reflective triangular highway warning devices to be displayed when necessary. Pull off the roadway as far as possible when changing flats or for other emergency situations. Turn on your vehicular hazard warning flashers when parked alongside a roadway, if only for a few minutes.

ADDITIONAL SAFETY CONSIDERATIONS. The operator is ultimately responsible for the safe operation of the vehicle. Improper operating procedures can jeopardize the safety of the occupants and others. The following suggest some procedures to help the operator enjoy safe, trouble free use.

☐Sanitize the fresh water supply system periodically. Keep fresh water in the potable water supply tank. Make sure that only sanitary water suitable for drinking is used to fill tank. Do not contaminate tank with water of questionable quality.

☐Keep water connection fittings from coming in contact with the ground or drain hose to reduce chance of contamination.

☐Never attempt to fix gas or electrical appliances yourself. Enlist services of a qualified technician.

☐Always have a serviceable fire extinguisher placed in an easily accessible location. This extinguisher should have a **rating of at least 4 BC units.**

☐ Check condition of smoke alarms regularly and immediately repair any that are not operating correctly.

☐ Don't overload your vehicle. Be careful not to cause an improper load distribution which can adversely affect roadability and/or towing safety.

☐ Ensure that tires are in good condition and are properly inflated. Watch inflation especially close on tandem axle models and on dual wheel models. Under-inflated tires run hotter and hot tires are more apt to blow out.

☐ Check and tighten wheel lugs regularly. Always keep lugs tight. Overtightening can cause distortion and breakage as well as prevent removal. Do not allow threads of lugs to become rusted.

☐ Check brakes in a safe area; not while traveling a busy highway.

☐ Always solidly chock trailer wheels before unhitching.

☐ Before leaving a camp area with a trailer in tow, make certain that the safety pin or locking lever is seated, breakaway wire is attached to tow vehicle and the electrical cord and safety chains are connected.

☐ Observe the warning labels attached to your RV concerning LP-Gas, water, electricity and loading.

☐ Do not operate the vehicle while under the influence of drugs or alcohol.

☐ NEVER store gasoline or diesel fuel in an area where fuel or fuel vapor may accumulate or may travel to an open spark.

WASTE DRAINAGE SYSTEM

GENERAL DESCRIPTION. Your waste drainage system was designed to provide adequate and safe storage and/or discharge of waste materials. All materials used in fabrication of the system and appliances and fixtures connected thereto are tested and approved by a nationally recognized testing laboratory. Installation of these materials is accomplished by approved methods. The entire fabricated waste system is factory tested in accordance with the American National Standards Code A119.2.

The drainage system basically uses properly sized ABS plastic piping and fittings connected to sinks, toilet and holding tanks and provides for their drainage to an outside termination. All fixtures incorporate the use of "P" traps or equivalent to provide a water seal against entry of sewer gases from outside connections. For fixed use, the RV should be reasonably level for best operation of the system.

WASTE HOLDING TANKS. The sewage or "black water" holding tank is located directly beneath the toilet. Before using, treat the tank with a gallon of water containing an odor control chemical such as "Aqua-Chem" or "Pink Magic". Place the recommended amount of chemical in the toilet. Be careful not to spill chemical on your hands, clothing or rug as it may cause an unremovable stain. Depress toilet pedal to allow mixing with toilet water. Continue to depress the pedal until approximately a gallon of water enters the waste tank. Release the pedal and the toilet waste tank is ready for use.

The "gray water" holding tank, if your RV is so equipped, will hold the sink and shower water. If your RV is parked and waste drain hose is connected, keep black water tank slide valve closed and open gray water tank slide valve. This will allow sink and shower water to drain away as it is used.

If your RV is not equipped with a "gray water" holding tank, sink and shower water will drain through the drain outlet (cap removed and drain hose connected).

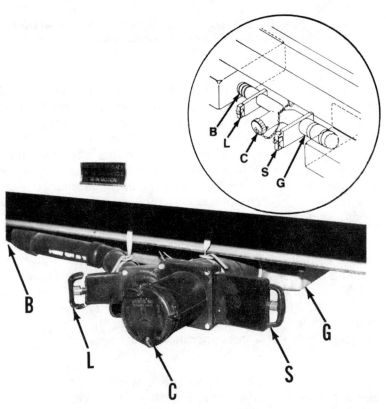

Views of typical "black water" and "gray water" holding tanks and slide valves.

B. Black water tank
C. Cap

G. Gray water tank

L. Large slide valve
S. Small slide valve

DRAIN OUTLET. The drain outlet is usually located on the left rear side. It is engineered for quick detachable type hookup of either the dust cap with attached chain or a drain hose adapter fitting. Always secure the cap when traveling to prevent any leakages.

DISPOSAL OF HOLDING TANK WASTES. Many states and parks have strict laws and regulations to prohibit dumping of wastes of any kind into other than regular disposal facilities or sewer systems. The dumping of raw sewage from toilet waste (black water) tanks into other than authorized facilities is universally prohibited.

Almost all privately owned parks have either a central dump facility or offer a campsite hook-up for sewage. By referring to Woodalls, Rand-McNally Camp Guide, Good Sam Camp Guide and various other good publications, you will find lists of many dump facilities throughout the U.S., Canada and Mexico. Plan ahead and you will have little inconvenience in proper disposal of wastes.

DUMPING THE WASTE HOLDING TANKS. Waste holding tanks are usually dumped while connected to a sewer rise at a travel park. You may find need to use other dump facilities from time to time. It is best to carry along various RV campground guides such as Woodalls, Rand McNally or Good Sam for their listing of dumping facilities. Holding tanks must be dumped only at approved disposal facilities.

Most of the unwanted solids build-up in the (black water) holding tank is due to using too little water and not flushing the tank out properly after each use. If you wish to dump a partially full tank, it is better to fill the remaining space in tank with water first to provide the volume necessary for complete flushing. Never use ammonias, alcohols or strong bleaches to clean the holding tank as they can cause damage to the plastic tank and drain lines.

Vehicle movement helps liquefy the solids for easier dumping of the tank. For this reason, when possible it is always better to dump soon after road travel rather than before road travel. To empty the tank, connect drain hose to the drain line termination fitting and the sewage receptor. Pull the "black water" slide valve in one slow continuous motion. After the tank empties, follow up with fresh water rinse. Close valve in one continuous motion and secure valve lever.

If your RV is equipped with a "gray water" holding tank, open the small slide valve and allow sink and shower water to drain. Close small valve, remove drain hose and secure dust cap.

POTABLE WATER SYSTEM

CITY WATER SYSTEM OPERATION. Connect a flexible hose with ¾-inch fittings to the city water service and the RV water filler fitting. Turn on city water and you will receive pressure at all faucets, toilet, the water storage tank and water heater. Some RV units have a city water inlet fitting separate from the storage tank. This inlet fitting is on the water system lines and check valves prevent storage tank from filling. Be sure to purge the system of trapped air before turning on the water heater.

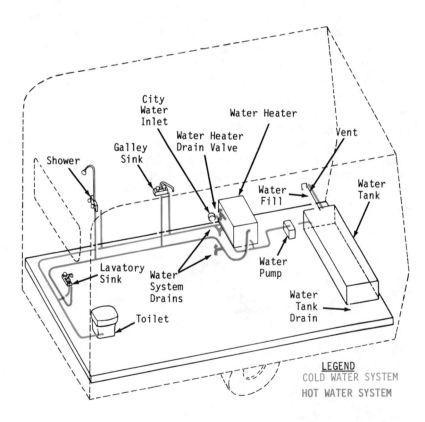

Schematic of a typical fresh water system.

⚠CAUTION

Excessive pressures from water supply systems may be encountered in some parks. If you RF is not so equipped, water pressure regulators are available to protect your system against such high pressure.

SANITIZING WATER SYSTEM. It is recommended that you completely sanitize the water system after delivery, after long periods of nonuse and after any suspected contamination. There are various commercial solutions approved for RV use available to assist you in sanitizing the system or you can use the one which follows:

Prepare a chlorine solution using one gallon of water and ¼-cup of household bleach (5% sodium hypochlorite solution). With water tank empty, pour one gallon of solution into tank for each 15 gallons of tank capacity. Complete filling of tank with fresh water. Open faucets to release air. Pressurize system with pump until water flows, then turn off pump and faucets. Allow to stand for three hours. Drain and flush with potable fresh water.

To remove excessive chlorine taste or odor which may remain, prepare a solution of one quart of vinegar to five gallons of water and allow solution to agitate in water tank by vehicle motion (several days if possible). Drain tank and again flush with potable fresh water.

USE OF WATER WHILE SELF-CONTAINED. It's hard to realize just how much water we use every day in normal home use. Newcomers to self-contained RVs soon discover that the water supply doesn't last long unless water conservation procedures are used. You can drastically reduce water consumption for showers by first wetting down and turning off the shower head, soaping yourself, then turning on the shower to rinse off. Once used to this practice, you'll find that a good shower only requires about a gallon. There will be plenty of water to meet your actual needs once you adjust your water use habits.

USING WATER SYSTEM DURING FREEZING WEATHER. Please keep in mind that most RVs are not designed for extended use during sub-freezing weather. However, with the addition of heat tapes on hoses, additional insulation, storm windows and with observance of certain procedures and physical limitations of equipment and design, you may be able to operate satisfactorily if temperatures do not drop too low.

Water freezes at any temperature below 32°F., but the real problems of RV operation come at bitterly cold temperatures. The interior water lines, water fixtures, water storage tank and pump assembly are normally protected from moderate freezing temperatures as long as the living area remains heated; however, drain lines exposed under the vehicle, may freeze quickly.

During freezing temperature it is important to winterize all systems as outlined on page 86 and following to prevent damage, even if RV is not being used.

WATER LINE DRAINS. Water system drains are located under the RV (various locations for different models) so that water lines may be purged of water for sanitizing, storage or winterization. Normally the water heater has a separate drain.

PHYSICAL PROTECTION OF INTERIOR WATER LINES. It is only human nature for all of us to "pack along" more of everthing than we actually need. Because of this, we tend to "stuff" things into almost every conceivable place, sometimes in places where we shouldn't. Be careful not to store heavy items such as canned goods, tools, etc., in areas where thay may come in contact with water piping and cause damage due to road vibration and shifting of the load. Leave plenty of space around the pump to allow operation.

LP-GAS SYSTEM

GENERAL DESCRIPTION. As with other systems in your RV, all components have been tested and approved for use in recreational vehicles by a nationally recognized testing laboratory. When properly handled. LP-Gas will provide you with trouble free operation of your heat producing appliances.

LP-Gas (liquefied petroleum) is a material composed of various hydrocarbons such as propane, propylene, butane, butylenes or a mixture of them. In its gaseous form (vaporized), it is colorless and carries an added garlic-like odor for detection. Besides being inflammable, it is potentially lethal to inhale, LP-Gas is compressed into a liquid form for storage and transportation. It is also known as bottle gas. Propane gas will vaporize during extreme cold (above − 44°F.), while butane will not vaporize below + 30°F. Most LP-Gas fueling stations sell only propane for RV use.

⚠WARNING

LP-Gas containers shall not be placed or stored inside the vehicle. LP-Gas containers are equipped with safety devices which relieve excessive pressure by discharging gas to the atmosphere.

The LP-Gas tank(s) mounted on your vehicle contains LP-fuel in liquid form under high pressure. As fuel is used, LP vapor passes from the top of the tank through a regulator which reduces the pressure to about 6½ ounces per square inch. Vapor at the low pressure is then transferred through the gas distribution lines for appliance use.

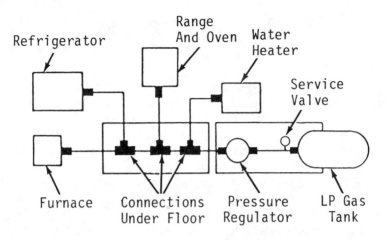

Drawing showing a typical LP-Gas distribution system.

Cooking appliances need fresh air for safe operation. Before operation:

1. Open overhead vent or turn on exhaust fan, and

2. Open window.

WARNING
IT IS NOT SAFE TO USE COOKING APPLIANCES FOR COMFORT HEATING

A warning label may be located in the cooking area to remind you to provide an adequate supply of fresh air for combustion. Unlike homes, the amount of oxygen supply is limited due to the size of the recreational vehicle, and proper ventilation when using the cooking appliance(s) will avoid dangers of asphyxiation. It is especially important that cooking appliances not be used for comfort heating as the danger of asphyxiation is greater when the appliance is used for long periods of time.

CHECKING FOR LEAKS. Upon delivery and periodically thereafter, check your gas system for possible leaks. Although the entire distribution system and its attached appliances have undergone extensive factory testing for leaks, with normal use being subject to road vibrations, connections and fittings can develop leaks. Usually you can detect these leaks by the strong odor of garlic or onions. If you do encounter this odor, turn off all open flames immediately and commence a systematic search for leaks throughout the gas system. Use a bubble solution or soapy water (NEVER A MATCH) on connections and fittings. Bubbles will appear at the leaky points. When tightening connections, use two wrenches with opposing torque to prevent twisting of copper tubing. If the leak doesn't show up in the manifold or copper tubing distribution system, then check the appliances.

NOTE

When the fuel level in an LP tank gets low, sometimes there is a concentration of garlic-like odor which may be mistaken for a gas leak. After changeover to a full tank, the odor usually will soon disappear.

IF YOU SMELL GAS

1. Extinguish any open flames, pilot lights and all smoking materials.

2. Do not touch electrical switches.

3. Shut off the gas supply at the tank valve(s) or gas supply connection.

4. Open doors and other ventilating openings.

5. Leave the area until odor clears.

6. Have the gas system checked and leakage source corrected before using again.

LP-Gas regulators must always be installed with the diaphragm vent facing downward. Regulators that are not in compartments have been equipped with a protective cover. Make sure that regulator vent faces downward and that cover is kept in place to minimize vent blockage which could result in excessive gas pressure causing fire or explosion.

LP-GAS REGULATOR SETTING. Never attempt to reset the gas regulator yourself. Have an authorized service agency make any regulator adjustments. Even a little amount of pressure over the recommended 6½ ounces per square inch can cause damage to appliance regulators.

AUTOMATIC CHANGEOVER REGULATOR. Your RV may be equipped with an automatic changeover regulator. This regulator allows both gas tanks to be turned on simultaneously. The arrow on the regulator handle indicates which tank is in service. When the indicated tank in service becomes empty, changeover is automatically accomplished to commence drawing fuel from the other tank. At this time, the plastic window will display a red signal or flag to indicate the automatic changeover condition. Upon first notice of this, you should then flip the lever over to indicate service on the other tank. The empty tank can then be turned off, uncoupled and taken to be refilled without disrupting the RV gas supply. After refilling the tank, it can be remounted and the shut-off valve turned on. When the other tank is depleted, the LP-Gas supply will again be automatically switched over.

FILLING LP-GAS TANKS. LP-Gas is available throughout the country. When one tank is depleted, it is best to have it refilled without delay. Woodalls, Rand-McNally and other good publications have listings of LP-Gas stations. Many travel parks have LP-Gas available.

⚠WARNING

Your RV may be equipped with exterior combustion air inlets. Appliance pilot lights should be turned off during gasoline or LP-Gas refueling on the unit.

⚠WARNING

LP-Gas containers should never be placed or stored inside the vehicle. LP-Gas containers are equipped with safety devices which relieve excessive pressure by discharging gas to the atmosphere.

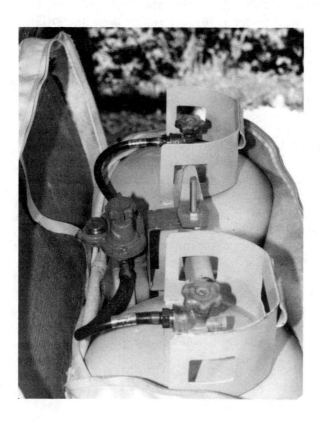

There are two basically different types of LP-Gas storage tanks. One type is made as specified by the Department Of Transportation and must be mounted upright. The D.O.T. tanks are often mounted at the front of trailers or in a compartment which is accessible only from outside the RV. These D.O.T. tanks should be removed while filling and are filled by weight. Information is stamped on the collar at top of tank to assist in filling.

The second type of storage tank is manufactured to specifications of the American Society of Mechanical Engineers. The A.S.M.E. tanks are mounted horizontally, usually under the RV and often only the valves, fittings and brackets are visible. Installation of the A.S.M.E. tanks are permanent. The tank is filled by volume and the tank is not removed for filling.

Permanent A.S.M.E. tanks are designed to be filled by volume as determined by the liquid level bleed (2). Tank is filled through valve (F). Refer to previous illustration for remainder of legend.

A warning label may be located near the LP-Gas container that reads:

WARNING
DO NOT FILL CONTAINER(S) TO MORE THAN 80
PERCENT OF CAPACITY

Overfilling the LP-Gas container can result in uncontrolled gas flow which can cause fire or explosion. A properly filled container will contain approximately 80 percent of its volume as liquid LP-Gas.

Portable fuel-burning equipment, including wood and charcoal grills and stoves, shall not be used inside the recreational vehicle. The use of this equipment inside the recreational vehicle may cause fires or asphyxiation.

Do not bring or store LP-Gas containers, gasoline or other flammable liquids inside the vehicle because a fire or explosion may result.

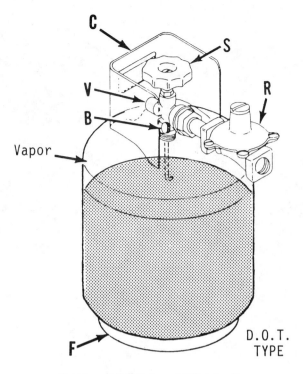

Drawing of D.O.T. type LP-Gas tank.

B. Bleed valve (10% or 20%)
C. Collar
F. Foot ring

R. Regulator
S. Service (main shut-off) valve
V. Relief valve

When removing or replacing either type of storage tank, remember that fuel line nuts at tanks are left hand thread. A clockwise force will loosen and counterclockwise will tighten the line nut. When tightening the line to tank nut, draw the nut up snug, but do not overtighten.

When LP-Gas tanks are filled to the proper level, there is available space for safe expansion of the vaporized liquid. Most tanks are equipped with 10% or 20% bleed valves (B). This valve is normally opened during filling and will indicate when tank is filled to proper limit by appearance of liquid replacing vapor. At all other times, the bleed valve should be tightly clos-

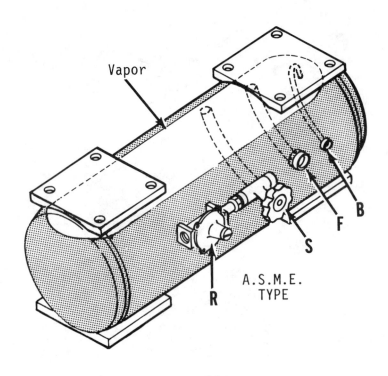

Vapor

A.S.M.E.
TYPE

R   F   B   S

ed by hand. Do not use pliers to close this valve. If your tank is overfilled and is not allowed to "bleed off" before installation with the RV system, it may gain pressure due to exposure to hot sun rays and will begin "blowing off" pressure from the relief valve (V). This can be detected by the strong odor around tanks and can be heard close up. Keep all open flames away from this area. It is best to remove the bottle, take it to a safe area and bleed off excess pressure by opening the main valve and closing it when discharge has been sufficient.

The main valve (S) on the LP-Gas tank should be tightened by hand only, using caution not to overtighten. The valve is designed to satisfactorily close with only a reasonable amount of tightening. Continual overtightening will eventually damage the valve and will require its replacement.

LP-GAS CONSUMPTION. Most gas appliances are only intermittently operated. Unless there is heavy use of hot water, water heater consumption is not too great. Operating under wintery conditions, requiring heavy use of the furnace or doing a lot of oven baking for hours at a time is what really consumes the gas rapidly. During freezing weather and high wind conditions, furnace consumption can be extremely heavy.

LP-Gas consumption depends upon individual use of appliances and the length of time operated. Each gallon of LP-Gas produces about 91500 BTU's of heat energy. A typical seven gallon container will provide about 640500 BTU's of heat energy. Following is a list of typical appliance consumption when turned full on for one hour of operation:

Appliance	Heavy Consumption
Water heater	8500 BTU
Refrigerator	1350 BTU
Furnace	30000 BTU
Range oven	10000 BTU
Each range top burner	5000 BTU

LP-GAS APPLIANCES

APPLIANCE SAFETY SHUT-OFF. Some LP-Gas appliances are equipped with a safety shut-off device that will shut off the gas supply to the appliance in the event the pilot flame is extinguished. Before the pilot can be relighted, the shut-off device must be reset. Turn control valve off and wait 5 minutes to allow any gas which may have accumulated in the burner compartment to escape before attempting to relight the pilot.

WATER HEATER OPERATION. If hot water is used with some discretion, there is always an ample supply for an entire family. With controls similar to those on your home water heater, LP-Gas is automatically supplied to heat water to a desired temperature and then automatically shut off, leaving the pilot burning. A regulated mixture of gas and air is ignited by the pilot to provide a flame which is directed into the heating tube. The heating assembly is sealed off from the RV interior and is vented to the outside atmosphere.

If gas supply to the water heater is cut off for any reason or if the pilot is blown out, all gas supply is automatically cut off and controls will have to be reset to obtain pilot relighting.

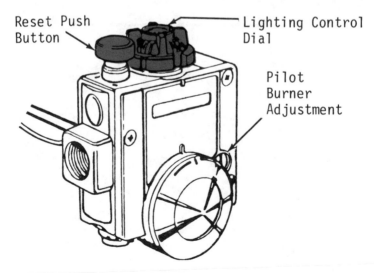

Reset Push Button

Lighting Control Dial

Pilot Burner Adjustment

A temperature and pressure relief valve is installed on your water heater. This relief valve is designed to open if the temperature of the water within the heater reaches 210°F or if water pressure in the heater reaches 150 psi. RV water systems are closed systems during the water heating cycle, the pressure build-up in the water sytem will reach 150 psi. When this pressure is reached, the pressure relief valve will open and water will drip from the valve. This dripping will continue until the pressure is reduced below 150 psi and valve closes. This condition is normal and does not indicate a defective relief valve. DO NOT plug, cap or reduce the outlet of the temperature and pressure relief valve.

LIGHTING THE WATER HEATER. Before lighting the water heater, make certain that the fresh water system is filled with water and the air is purged from the water heater by opening all faucets until water flows steadily from each.

⚠CAUTION

Damage may result from operating water heater when system is not filled with water.

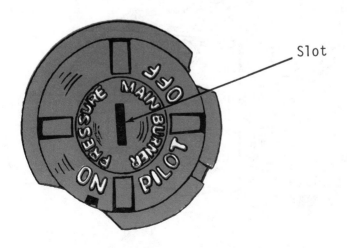

Slot

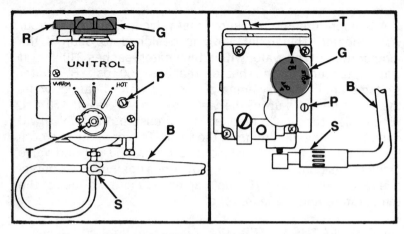

View showing typical LP-Gas water heater control valves.

B. Burner
G. Control dial

P. Pilot adjustment
R. Reset button

S. Air shutter
T. Temperature dial

Temperature Selection Lever

Lighting/Control (Reset) Dial

Pressure Regulator Adjustment

Pilot Gas Adjustment Cover Screw

To light, turn the gas cock knob (G) to the "OFF" position. Wait 5 minutes to allow gas which may have accumulated in the burner compartment to escape. Turn gas cock dial to "Pilot" position. Depress and hold reset button (R) while lighting pilot flame. Allow pilot to burn for about 30 seconds before releasing the reset button. If pilot does not remain lighted, repeat operation allowing longer period before releasing reset button. Turn gas cock dial to "ON" position. Turn temperature dial (T) to desired temperature setting.

PILOT FLAME. If the pilot flame does not have a small yellow tip, the pilot is not receiving enough gas. A large yellow flame indicates too much gas supply. If necessary, adjust the pilot as follows:

Remove pilot adjustment cap at right front face of water heater control to reveal the adjustment screw (P). Turn adjustment screw clockwise to reduce gas flow and counterclockwise to increase gas flow. Adjust pilot until a slight yellow tip appears on a ½-inch flame as shown. Reinstall pilot adjustment cap.

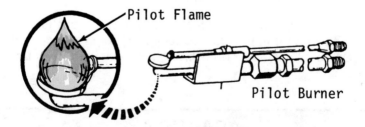

WATER HEATER PILOT ADJUSTMENT

View of typical pilot flame on LP-Gas water heater. Turn pilot screw (P in previous illustration) for adjustment.

Main burner air shutter adjustment of LP-Gas water heater. Refer to text for procedure.

BURNER FLAME. If main burner flame is yellow and causing soot deposits, loosen retaining screw and open the air shutter on burner until signs of yellow flame is gone. Retighten shutter screw. If shutter is opened too far and allows too much air to enter burner, blue flame will be noisy and will burn with a space between flame and burner.

Make certain that the water heater service door is firmly secured. The vent in this door is necessary for proper combustion. Do not block the air flow through the vent with any form of windshield.

⚠CAUTION

Open a window or vent and use the range exhaust fan to remove humidity and odors produced by cooking.

RANGE/OVEN. The range and oven combination or counter-top range and wall oven have been certified by a nationally recognized testing laboratory such as the American Gas Association or Underwriters Laboratories.

⚠WARNING

IT IS NOT SAFE TO USE COOKING APPLIANCES FOR COMFORT HEATING.

Cooking appliances need fresh air for safe operation. Before operation:
1. Open overhead vent or turn on exhaust fan, and
2. Open window.

A warning label may be located in the cooking area to remind you to provide an adequate supply of fresh air for combustion. Unlike homes, the amount of oxygen supply is limited

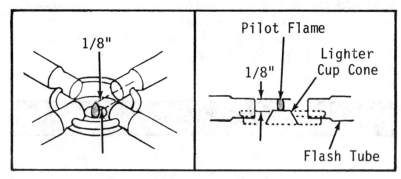

Views showing typical range top burner pilot flame adjustment.

due to the size of the recreational vehicle, and proper ventilation when using the cooking appliance(s) will avoid dangers of asphyxiation. It is especially important that cooking appliances not be used for comfort heating as the danger of asphyxiation is greater when the appliance is used for long periods of time.

Operational information and adjustments are as follows:

TOP BURNERS AND TOP PILOT. If so equipped, adjust top pilot so that tip of the pilot flame is just over the edge of the inner cone as shown. Burners should light within four seconds. If lighting is difficult, air shutter on burner may be set too far open. Air shutters on top burners should be adjusted so that each cone of the flame is separate and distinct with no yellow tips. If air shutters are set too far open, the flame will lift away from the burner head, will be difficult to light and may flash back into the air mixture chamber. If air shutters are set too far closed, the flame will look hazy with yellowing tips.

OVEN AND PILOT. The oven thermostat does not have a bypass setting. It will cycle on and off at all temperature settings except broil. The oven control knob is combined with the constant pilot shut-off. For normal use turn control knob only between "Off" and "Broil". When traveling turn control knob to "Pilot Off". To relight, turn control from "Pilot Off" to "Off" and light pilot with a match.

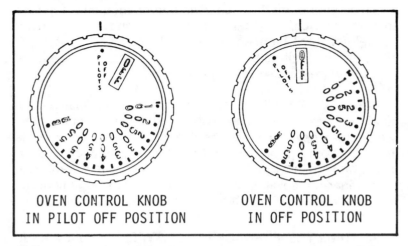

OVEN CONTROL KNOB
IN PILOT OFF POSITION

OVEN CONTROL KNOB
IN OFF POSITION

Oven control knobs in "Pilots Off" (left) and "Off" (right) positions. Refer to text.

NOTE

On some models, the top burner pilot is also turned off and on by the oven control knob. If so equipped always relight top pilot when relighting oven pilot.

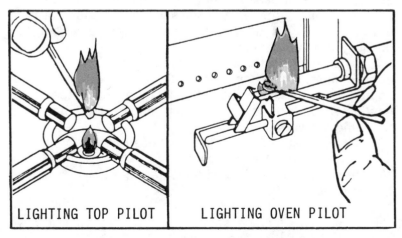

LIGHTING TOP PILOT

LIGHTING OVEN PILOT

Light top pilot and oven pilot with a match.

The air shutter on the oven main burner should be adjusted so that each cone of flame is separate and distinct. If air shutter is set too far open, flame will be noisy and tend to lift off the ports. If air shutter is set too far closed, flame will be yellow and may cause soot formation.

FURNACE OPERATION. The furnace utilizes a sealed combustion system. The combustion chamber is completely sealed from the inner atmosphere of the RV. Combustion air is drawn in from the outside and combustion products are expelled outside through the vent. The system is very stable and even under the severest of wind conditions, it is almost impossible for the flame to blow out.

LIGHTING THE FURNACE (PILOT TYPE). To light the furnace, make certain LP-Gas is available to furnace and proceed as follows:

1. Remove furnace front panel.
2. Set furnace thermostat to highest setting.
3. Turn gas control valve knob to "Off" position and wait five minutes.
4. Reset thermostat to "Off" setting.
5. Turn gas valve knob to "Pilot" position.
6. Depress gas valve knob and light pilot by depressing ignitor. Several strokes of ignitor may be required before pilot will ignite. Some early models without ignition button must be lit manually with a match through a front opening at pilot light location.
7. When pilot continues to burn, hold the knob in for approximately 30 seconds or until the pilot remains lighted when it is released. If pilot goes out, repeat lighting Steps 2 through 7 allowing longer time before releasing gas valve knob.
8. Turn gas valve knob to full "On" position.
9. Reinstall furnace front panel.
10. Set thermostat at desired temperature. Furnace will now operate automatically.

For complete furnace shut-down, turn gas control valve knob to "Off" position and thermostat to "Off" setting.

LIGHTING THE FURNACE (AUTOMATIC IGNITION TYPE).

This furnace has a direct spark ignition system and has no pilot light. To place furnace in operation, proceed as follows:

1. Remove furnace front panel.
2. Turn manual gas valve to "Off" position.
3. Set thermostat above actual temperature to operate blower. Allow blower to operate for five minutes.
4. Set thermostat to "Off".
5. Turn gas valve to full "On" position.
6. Set thermostat at desired temperature (must be above room temperature for furnace to ignite). Allow 30 seconds for burner to light. Burner flame can be observed through observation hole.

If burner does not light, set thermostat to "Off" and repeat ignition procedure. If after three attempts, there is still no ignition, completely shut down the furnace and determine the cause.

For complete furnace shut-down, turn manual gas valve "Off" and set thermostat to "Off" position.

GAS/ELECTRIC REFRIGERATOR OPERATION.

All Gas/Electric refrigerators operate with ammonia-water mixture absorption systems. In the boiler, ammonia vapor is distilled from the ammonia-water mixture and is carried to the finned condenser, where it liquifies. The liquid flows to the evaporator, where it creates cold by evaporating into a circulating flow of hydrogen gas. If the evaporator coil is not level, the liquid readily accumulates, forming pockets which can impair the gas circulation or even block it. In this case, the cooling will stop. When the RV is stationary, it should be leveled to be comfortable to live in. If the refrigerator is properly installed (freezer shelf parallel to floor), the refrigerator will then also perform well. A bubble level should be placed on the freezer shelf to check refrigerator for levelness.

When refrigerator is switched to electric operation, ammonia-water mixture is heated by a heating element instead of the burner flame.

Although there are several manufacturers of Gas/Electric refrigerators, the following paragraphs covering some Dometic and Norcold models will give you a general knowledge of the controls and operation of Gas/Electric refrigerators.

DOMETIC (EARLY) 3-WAY OPERATION. The 3-way design uses LP-Gas, 120 volt AC or 12 volt DC electricity for power. The control panel is located inside the refrigerator.

For LP-Gas operation, turn the OFF/12V/ELEC/GAS selector counterclockwise to GAS. Pull the valve button out while pushing lighter button in. Repeat this until ignition is observed through the reflector. Turn the gas thermostat to the highest number on the dial. Later adjust temperature to meet your cooling requirements.

For electric operation when 120 volt AC power cord is connected, switch the refrigerator selector knob to ELEC setting. Turn electric thermostat to highest number on the dial. Later adjust the setting downward to meet your cooling needs.

For 12 volt DC electric operation, switch the refrigerator selector knob to the 12V setting. Power is now furnished by the RV battery. Turn electric thermostat to highest number on the dial. Later adjust setting downward to meet your cooling needs.

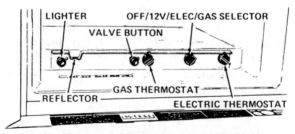

3-WAY REFRIGERATOR CONTROLS

View showing 3-way controls of early Dometic Gas/Electric refrigerator.

DOMETIC (EARLY) 2-WAY OPERATION. The 2-way design operates on LP-Gas or 120 volt AC electricity.

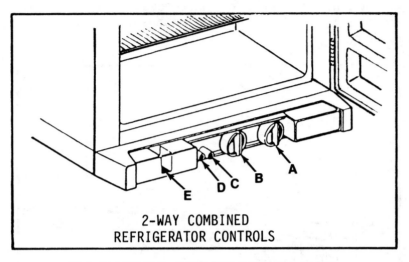

2-WAY COMBINED
REFRIGERATOR CONTROLS

Early Dometic 2-way Gas/Electric refrigerator controls.

A. Selector knob
B. Thermostat
C. Pilot gas button
D. Piezo lighter button
E. Reflector

For LP-Gas operation, turn selector knob (A) to GAS position. Turn thermostat knob (B) to setting 4. Hold inward on button (C) and push Piezo lighter button (D) several times until the burner flame can be seen in reflector (E). After burner ignites, continue holding inward on button (C) for 10 seconds. Release button (C) and check in reflector to be sure burner is still lit. If flame is out, repeat the lighting procedure. Later, adjust thermostat (B) to a setting that meets your cooling needs.

For 120 volt AC electric operation, turn selector knob (A) to ELEC position. Turn thermostat (B) to setting 4. Later, adjust thermostat (B) to a setting that meets your cooling needs.

DOMETIC (LATE) AES OPERATION. This refrigerator is equipped with an automatic energy selector system. The control system selects the most suitalble available energy source.

The selection will be made with highest priority to 120 volt AC. Second priority to 12 volt DC and the lowest priority to LP-Gas operation. No manual operation is necessary for change of energy. If the refrigerator does not succeed in lighting the gas, the lamp (E) will change from continuous green to a flashing red light.

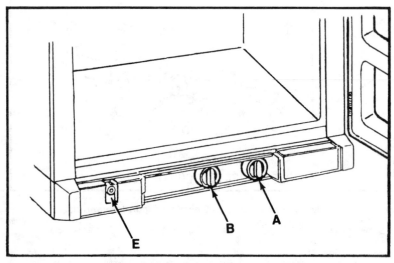

Late Dometic automatic energy selector controls on Gas/Electric refrigerator.
A. ON-OFF switch   B. Thermostat   E. Indicator

Before starting the refrigerator, check to be sure all gas valves are turned on and that the unit is level. Turn knob (A) to "On" position. Lamp (E) should now be green. Turn thermostat (B) to setting 4. Later adjust thermostat to a setting that meets your cooling needs.

If battery voltage drops, the control system will start continuous gas operation. The thermostat will not be in operation. When the voltage increases, normal operation will start up again.

NORCOLD (MODEL EG2) OPERATION. Model EG2 refrigerators are designed to operate on LP-Gas or 120 volt AC energy sources. However, a 12 volt DC supply must be con-

nected to energize the direct spark system to light the gas burner. Refer to various views of the electronic mode selector.

LIGHTING INSTRUCTIONS — GAS MODE

START UP INSTRUCTIONS — ELECTRIC MODE

SHUT DOWN INSTRUCTIONS — GAS OR ELECTRIC

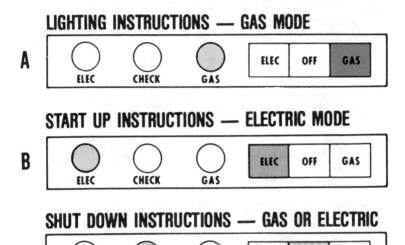

Various views of the Norcold Model EG2 Gas/Electric refrigerator electronic mode selector. Refer to text.

To operate refrigerator in the gas mode, turn thermostat to mid-range setting. Refer to (view A) and depress switch to "GAS" position. Sparking will start at burner and gas valve will open. Blue light indicates the refrigerator is in the gas mode. (If blue light does not come on, check for loss of 12 volt DC supply). After 10 seconds, the burner should be ignited and operating normally. On the initial start-up of refrigerator in gas mode, it may take longer than 10 seconds to allow air to be purged from gas line. If the gas does not ignite within 10 seconds, gas valve will automatically shut off and the red (check) light will come on. To restart when the check light is on, depress switch to "OFF" position. Wait 10 seconds and depress switch to "GAS" position.

To operate the refrigerator in the electric mode, make certain the 120 volt AC supply is connected to refrigerator. Turn thermostat to mid-range setting. Refer to (view B) and depress switch to "ELEC" position. Green light will indicate the refrigerator is operating properly in the electric mode. If the green light comes on regardless of switch setting, check for reverse polarity at 120 volt receptacles.

To shut down refrigerator, refer to (view C) and depress selector switch to "OFF" position. All indicator lights will be off.

LIGHTING INSTRUCTIONS — GAS MODE

A

| DC/GAS | OFF | AC | | DC | AC | CHECK | GAS | | ELEC | GAS |

START UP INSTRUCTIONS — AC MODE

B

| DC/GAS | OFF | AC | | DC | AC | CHECK | GAS | | ELEC | GAS |

START UP INSTRUCTIONS — DC MODE

C

| DC/GAS | OFF | AC | | DC | AC | CHECK | GAS | | ELEC | GAS |

SHUT DOWN INSTRUCTIONS — GAS OR ELECTRIC

D

| DC/GAS | OFF | AC | | DC | AC | CHECK | GAS | | ELEC | GAS |

Various views of the Norcold Model EG3 Gas/Electric refrigerator electronic mode selector. Refer to text.

NORCOLD (MODEL EG3) OPERATION. Model EG3 refrigerators are designed to operate on LP-Gas, 120 volt AC or 12 volt DC electricity. The 12 volt DC supply must be connected to energize the direct spark ignition system for LP-Gas operation. Refer to various views of the electronic mode selector.

To operate refrigerator in the gas mode, turn thermostat to mid-range setting. Refer to (view A) and depress the selector switch to "GAS" position. Depress the DC/GAS-OFF-AC switch to "DC/GAS" position. Sparking will start at burner and gas valve will open. Blue light indicates the refrigerator is in the gas mode. (If blue light does not come on, check for loss of 12 volt DC supply). After 10 seconds, the burner should be ignited and operating normally. On the initial refrigerator start-up, it may take longer than 10 seconds to allow air to be purged from the gas line. If the gas does not ignite within 10 seconds, gas valve will automatically shut off and the red (check) light will come on. To restart when the red (check) light is on, depress the DC/GAS-OFF-AC switch to "Off" position. Wait 10 seconds, then depress switch again to "DC/GAS" position.

To operate the refrigerator in the 120 volt AC mode, make certain the 120 volt AC power cord is connected. Turn thermostat to mid-range setting. Refer to (view B) and depress selector switch to "ELEC" position. Depress DC/GAS-OFF-AC switch to "AC" position. Green light will indicate the refrigerator is operating properly in the AC mode. If the green light comes on regardless of the switch settings, check for reverse polarity at 120 volt receptacles.

To operate the refrigerator in the 12 volt DC mode, make certain the 12 volt supply is available to refrigerator. Turn thermostat to mid-range setting. Refer to (view C) and depress selector switch to "ELEC" position. Depress DC/GAS-OFF-AC switch to "DC/GAS" position. Amber light will indicate the refrigerator is operating properly in the DC mode.

To shut down the refrigerator, refer to (view D) and depress the DC/GAS-OFF-AC switch to "OFF" position. All indicator lights will be off.

ELECTRICAL SYSTEM

GENERAL DESCRIPTION. The electrical system may vary between types and models of RV units. On some models, the system is designed to provide power to your appliances and lights from either a 120 volt AC outside source or a 12 volt DC battery installed in your RV. The 12 volt battery will recharge while your RV is connected to the 120 volt source or when driving if equipped with a charge line to your automotive alternator. As with all other RV systems, the electrical equipment has been installed in an approved manner required by the American National Standard A119.2.

Remember that the power from the battery is limited. You will find from experience just about how long the battery will last before it needs recharging.

CHANGES, MODIFICATIONS AND ADDITIONS. Your electrical system of 120 volts AC or 12 volts DC has been designed and installed in accordance with the safety requirements of

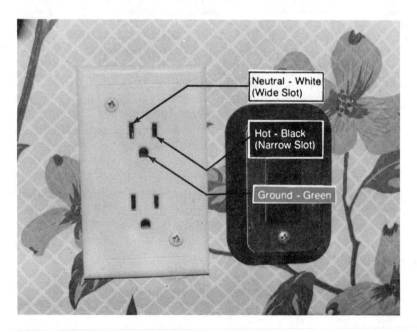

ANSI Standard A119.2 and the National Electrical Code ANSI/NFPA70. Any changes, additions and/or modifications that you make after delivery may develop a hazardous condition. Be sure to consult your local authorized dealer for advice concerning changes or additions. Only qualified electrical technicians should attempt to make any changes or additions to your electrical system, and then using only approved materials and components and employing approved methods of installation.

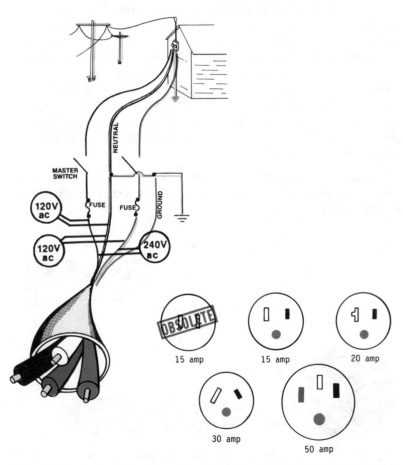

National Electric Code Requirements specify that 120 volt AC receptacles and plugs be wired as shown.

CONNECTING TO 120 VOLT AC SOURCE. The 120 volt power in your RV is carried by the heavy duty 30 amp power cord when it is connected to a 120 volt power source (house, camp-ground, etc.). It supplies current to the 120 volt receptacles and appliances. It also supplies current to the 12 volt lights inside and any 12 volt receptacles through the use of a power converter. The 120 volt system is protected by a circuit breaker box. The most common cause of an open circuit breaker is an overloaded circuit.

The heavy duty 30 amp power cord is equipped with a 30 amp plug having pins arranged as shown. The third pin is a means of connecting the exposed metal parts of appliances or the recreational vehicle to earth ground so there can be no voltage difference between them to cause an electrical shock. The metal skin of an RV must be bonded to the metal frame. The frame, water pipes, gas pipes and all other exposed metal parts must be connected to the grounding bus in the circuit breaker box (distribution panel). The grounding bus is then connected through the green wire in the power supply cord to the third pin. The third pin in the park receptacle is then connected to earth ground.

If you must plug into a receptacle with no provision for the third pin, use an adapter with a pigtail that can be connected to the receptacle box.

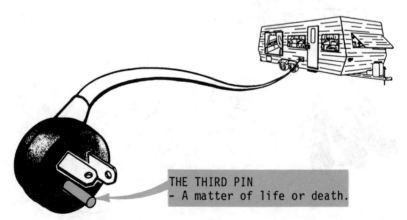

THE THIRD PIN
- A matter of life or death.

The round, third pin on your 120 volt AC power supply cord is the safety ground pin.

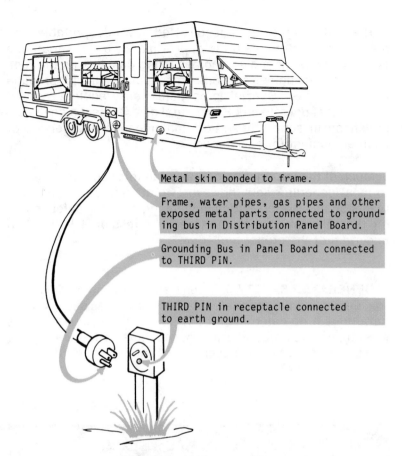

Metal skin bonded to frame.

Frame, water pipes, gas pipes and other exposed metal parts connected to grounding bus in Distribution Panel Board.

Grounding Bus in Panel Board connected to THIRD PIN.

THIRD PIN in receptacle connected to earth ground.

View showing a typical safety ground connection.

AUXILIARY GENERATOR. Some models may be equipped with a gasoline engine powered auxiliary generator which supplies 120 volt AC power. The unit may be built into a compartment of the trailer or motorhome, use fuel from the motorhome main supply tank and be permanently wired into the system. Additionally separate portable generator sets may be used to deliver 120 volt AC power when recreational vehicle is located in a remote area. Similar precautions should be taken regardless of type.

The following section is directed towards portable and standby generator sets up to approximately 8 kw output. The section covers air-cooled engines using gasoline as the fuel. Generator set engines are sometimes fueled using LP/propane or natural gas. Special procedures are required around engines that operate on LP or natural gas. Contact a dealer experienced in set-up, operation, maintenance and service of such equipment for assistance.

Much of the information contained in this section will apply to most generator sets, however, variations do exist and the reader should exercise good judgement, heed the safety notes on the following pages, and seek professional help when uncertain of the proper procedure.

GENERATOR SAFETY. The generator is an engine-driven device designed to produce electric current, and as such, may be hazardous if operated improperly. In addition, generators are sometimes used around utility service lines and the operator must be aware of their presence and exercise caution to prevent electric shock.

⚠DANGER

Stop generator or switch off current when working on or around any wiring. Generators and house wiring can produce sufficient electric current to cause death. Follow safe procedures to prevent electric shock.

All electric-powered equipment should be U.L. listed. The Underwriters Laboratory (U.L.) listing on the label indicates the products electrical system has been tested and found safe for recommended applications. Equipment manufacturers urge buyers also to use U.L. listed extension cords for safer operation.

HELPFUL HINT

Wire sizes are usually given as a number followed by "gage" or "gauge". Smaller numbers are actually larger diameter wire sizes. As an example, 10 gage wire is larger than 14 gage, which is larger than 16 gage.

SAFETY HINT

Heat is an indication that something is wrong. The problem may be improper operation, a bad connection or a faulty part. Stop and investigate anytime excessive heat is noticed. Hot spot along extension cord probably indicates a broken wire. Cords often break near the ends where they are flexed a lot. If equipment (especially around motor) gets very hot, the motor may be damaged, but probably cooling air circulation is restricted or the unit is overloaded.

Observe the following check list **in addition to STANDARD SAFETY PRACTICES.**

1. Don't touch electrical equipment when standing in water or on wet ground or with wet hands.

2. Stop generator or disconnect power source when inspecting or working on electrical equipment.

3. When practicable, keep one hand in a pocket while inspecting or working on live electrical equipment or circuits.

4. All wiring must meet all state and local electrical codes. All wiring and electrical equipment installations must be performed by a licensed electrician if stipulated by electrical code.

5. Remove watches, rings and other jewelry when inspecting or working on electrical equipment.

6. Work methodically and thoughtfully. Don't take unnecessary risks.

7. Where applicable, generator must be grounded properly.

8. Know procedure for moving a victim away from electrical source and first aid procedure for treatment of electrical shock.

9. The generator set must be secured so it cannot slide or shift when operating.

10. All guards and shields must be in place during operation.

11. The area in which the generator set operates must be well-ventilated.

12. Always disconnect the spark plug lead and properly ground the lead before working on generator set.

13. Observe safety rules when charging a battery.

SELECTING THE RIGHT SIZE GENERATOR. Auxiliary or standby generators are available in many sizes, rated by watts or kilowatts (kw) output. The small 300-watt units are convenient, easily portable and less expensive than a larger model, but they will be at their maximum limit when operating three 100-watt light bulbs and they probably will not operate any heating appliances.

To calculate your requirements, check the power requirements of the pieces of electrical equipment you desire to operate, and then add the wattages. Light bulbs, electrical heaters and many small appliances use the same wattage to start as to run, but air conditioners, water pumps, air compressors, power saws, etc., may require six times the normal running power to start. It may be possible to stagger loads by alternating heavy demand appliances, especially those that re-

APPLIANCES	PRIORITY COMBINATIONS IN WATTS					
1. _____						
2. _____						
3. _____						
4. _____						
5. _____						
6. _____						
7. _____						
8. _____						
9. _____						
10. _____						
11. _____						
12. _____						
13. _____						
14. _____						
15. _____						

TOTAL MUST NOT EXCEED_____ *
WATTS PER COLUMN

*List capacity of generator set here.

quire high wattage for starting. However, it is always best to operate the generator with a load well below the maximum output.

The wattage listed on the data plate of each appliance should be used for calculations. If the rating on the data plate is in amperes, multiply the voltage times the amperage to find the watts (amperes x volts = watts). The table lists approximate wattages required by some popular appliances.

APPROXIMATE WATTAGE REQUIREMENTS

	approximate watts
Air conditioning*	1500-3000
Battery charger	100-500
Broiler oven**	1500
Chain saw	1200-2500
Coffe maker (large)	1100
Converter/Charger	700-1200
Fry pan	1500
Heater	500-1300
Hot plate**	1250
Iron	700-1500
Refrigerator	300-1000
Soldering iron	40-500
Television (B&W)	100-300
(Color)	300-600
Toaster (two-slice)	1100

*Depends upon BTU size.

**Most home type electrical heaters or large electrical broilers are not suitable for RV use due to excessive power requirements.

APPROXIMATE WATTAGE OF MOTORS

Motors	Start (Capacitor)	Run
1/6 hp	850	275
1/4 hp	1050	400
1/3 hp	1350	450
1/2 hp	1800	600
3/4 hp	2600	850
1 hp	3300	1100

STARTING BUILT IN GENERATORS. Before starting the generator, turn off all electrical appliances in the unit, make sure intake and exhaust outlets are free of obstructions and check the engine oil level. On some units, the power supply cord must be plugged into the generator receptacle; on other units the generator is wired directly to the breaker box. Depress the START/STOP switch to START and hold until the generator engine is running. When released the switch will return to neutral position.

To turn the generator off, press the START/STOP switch to STOP and hold until the generator stops running.

STARTING PORTABLE GENERATORS. Most generators of less than 10 kw output are powered by 2- or 4-stroke engines which use gasoline as fuel. Refer to the appropriate following section for starting procedure.

2-Stroke Models

The 2-stroke engine is lubricated by oil mixed with the fuel (gasoline). Follow the manufacturer's recommendation for oil type, gasoline type and fuel:oil ratio. If the manufacturer's recommendations are not available, contact your dealer. Don't guess when selecting oil, gasoline and fuel:oil ratio. Severe damage to a 2-stroke engine can occur as a result of running on a fuel mixture consisting of the wrong oil or gasoline, or a fuel mixture of the wrong fuel:oil ratio.

⚠WARNING

Gasoline is extremely flammable. DO NOT smoke or allow sparks or open flame around fuel or in presence of fuel vapor. Be sure area is well-ventilated. Wipe up spilled fuel immediately. Observe fire prevention rules.

Mix oil and gasoline in a suitable container; don't attempt to mix oil and gasoline in the engine's fuel tank.

DO NOT fill the fuel tank while the engine is running or if the engine is hot.

Disconnect or turn off any load connected to the generator before starting engine.

Some units are equipped with an idling device that sets engine speed at idle if there is no load. Some manufacturers recommend switching off the idling device when starting the engine.

Position the choke according to ambient and engine temperatures. A cold engine almost always needs full choke, while a warm or hot engine may require some or no choke. Each engine is a little different so experimentation may help. Start engine. If equipped with a rewind starter don't jerk the rope and don't pull to full extension. While holding handle, allow starter rope to slowly rewind; don't release so that handle impacts starter housing.

DO NOT JERK ROPE WHEN PULLING. REWIND SMOOTHLY.

If engine will not start within a reasonable period, refer to a maintenance/service manual or ask your dealer to check out operation of the generator set.

4-Stroke Models
Before starting a 4-stroke generator engine, check and be sure the engine lubricating oil level is correct. If uncertain of how to check oil level, ask your dealer or refer to a service manual. Oil level dipsticks are marked in various ways; be certain you are correctly reading the oil level.

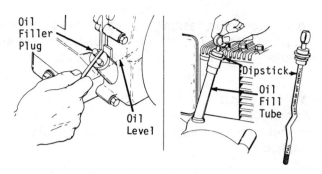

Fill the fuel tank with the manufacturer's recommended gasoline. DO NOT fill the tank if the engine is running or the engine is hot.

Disconnect or turn off any load connected to the generator before starting engine.

Some units are equipped with an idling device that sets engine speed at idle if there is no load. Some manufacturers recommend switching off the idling device when starting the engine.

Position the choke according to ambient and engine temperatures. A cold engine almost always needs full choke, while a warm or hot engine may require some or no choke. Each engine is different so experimentation may help. Start engine using electric starter or manual starter. Don't jerk rewind starter rope, if so equipped, and don't pull to full extension. While holding the handle, allow starter rope to slowly rewind; don't release so that handle will impact starter housing.

If equipped with an electric starter, don't engage starter for more than 30 seconds as starter may be damaged due to overheating.

If the generator set is designed with a battery to be used for electric starting, DO NOT attempt to manually start the engine with the battery disconnected from the generator set.

APPLYING A LOAD TO GENERATOR. Run the engine a few minutes before connecting or switching on the load. This will allow the engine to warm so it will not stumble or die when the load is applied.

Before connecting any load to the generator, check the data plate on the generator and be sure the load does not exceed the generator's capacity. Refer to SELECTING THE RIGHT SIZE GENERATOR for information on matching load to generator capacity. Be sure frequency and phase are also matched.

DO NOT exceed the current rating of the generator's outlets.

⚠CAUTION

DO NOT exceed generator capacity specified on generator data plate. Overloading may shorten life and cause internal damage to the generator and attached appliances. DO NOT exceed amperage rating of generator outlets.

Be aware that some electrical devices, particularly electric motors, require additional current for starting which may exceed the outlet receptacle's current rating. Refer to SELECTING THE RIGHT SIZE GENERATOR for some typical starting current requirements for capacitor start electric motors. Other types of electric motors may require more or less current for starting.

Apply multiple loads to the generator gradually. Connect the largest load first then connect smaller loads. If more than one receptacle is available, split the load as evenly as possible between receptacles.

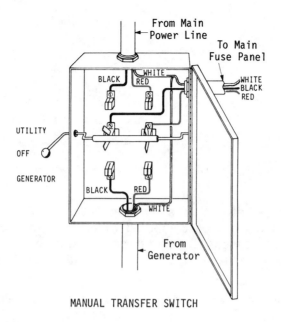

From Main
Power Line

To Main
Fuse Panel

BLACK   WHITE
RED

WHITE
BLACK
RED

UTILITY

OFF

GENERATOR

BLACK   RED

WHITE

From
Generator

MANUAL TRANSFER SWITCH

If the generator set is a standby unit, turn off or disconnect all electrical devices and start the generator before moving the transfer switch lever to "GENERATOR". Apply the largest load first followed by progressively smaller loads. Depending on the capacity of the generator, it is likely that the standby generator's capacity can be exceeded if all possible loads are applied to the circuit, especially if electric motors are started. Know the generator's capacity and only apply loads which will not exceed it.

120 VOLT DUPLEX RECEPTACLE

Single
Outlet

CAUTION
SEVERE DAMAGE TO
ALTERNATOR MAY
RESULT FROM THIS
TYPE CONNECTION

Single
Outlet

20 AMP
LOAD

120V-20A

Duplex
Receptacle

20 AMP

120V-20A

Duplex
Receptacle

INDIVIDUAL
LOAD ITEMS

20 AMP

Single
Outlet

Single
Outlet

PROPER CONNECTION OF A 20 AMP LOAD, MAXIMUM
RECEPTACLE RATING CAN BE OBTAINED
THRU A SINGLE OUTLET OR SPLIT BETWEEN EACH OUTLET

IMPROPER CONNECTION OF LOAD ITEMS
DUPLEX RECEPTACLE TOTAL LOAD EXCEEDS 20 AMPERES

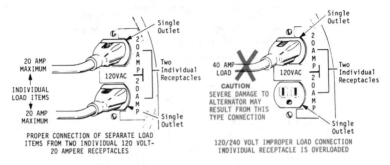

TWO INDIVIDUAL 120 VOLT RECEPTACLES

PROPER CONNECTION OF SEPARATE LOAD
ITEMS FROM TWO INDIVIDUAL 120 VOLT-
20 AMPERE RECEPTACLES

120/240 VOLT IMPROPER LOAD CONNECTION
INDIVIDUAL RECEPTACLE IS OVERLOADED

A load priority chart is provided on page 69 so various combinations may be computed which will not exceed the generator's capacity. Be sure to use the starting wattage for devices such as refrigerators that are equipped with an electric motor.

The generator set is designed to run at a certain speed, usually 3600 rpm. Generator speed must be maintained at design speed so the correct voltage is produced at the correct alternating current frequency.

⚠CAUTION

NEVER manipulate the throttle or governor mechanism when the generator set is running. Increasing engine speed may cause generator damage as well as damage to electric devices connected to generator.

STOPPING GENERATOR. Most manufacturers recommend that any load connected to the generator be disconnected in stages. This allows the engine to cool gradually. After all load is removed, run the engine from one to ten minutes before stopping, depending on the amount of load applied during operation.

After stopping, close the fuel shut-off valve, if so equipped, and perform whatever service is required based on the generator's use. Refer to the maintenance sections on the following pages.

Be aware that engine and its exhaust system will remain hot for period of time after the engine stop running. Care must be exercised when working on or around the hot engine and exhaust system.

GENERATOR ENGINE MAINTENANCE. Periodically the air and fuel filters should be inspected and cleaned or renewed if required. The recommended service interval varies according to engine manufacturer and operating environment. Contact your dealer or refer to a service manual for recommended service interval.

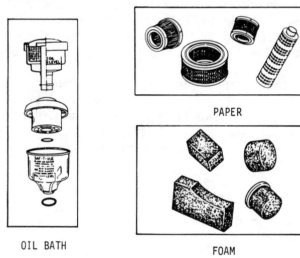

OIL BATH

PAPER

FOAM

Air filters used on generator engines are usually one of three types: foam, paper cartridge or oil bath. The foam type air filter is cleaned by washing in liquid soap and water. Squeeze the foam dry, lightly oil the foam with engine oil, then squeeze the foam to remove excess oil and distribute the oil through the foam. Dry type filters made of paper can only be cleaned by lightly tapping to dislodge dirt and debris, otherwise, paper filters must be renewed. Some dry type filters made of synthetic or metallic material can be cleaned by washing with soap and water; rinse and dry filter thoroughly before installing. Oil bath type filters use a reservoir of oil to entrap foreign particles. Service the oil bath filter by disassembling and cleaning filter components, then reassemble the filter while filling the reservoir with engine oil to the oil level mark.

Fuel filters may be located in the fuel tank or in the fuel line. Contaminated fuel filters should be renewed. If filter blockage is a persistent problem attempt to identify the source of the contaminant. Check the fuel tank for rust. Metal fuel tanks containing gasohol are particularly susceptible to rust over a period of time.

Generator engines are air-cooled. Periodically inspect the engine's cooling fins and remove any debris or other material which may block air movement. It may be necessary to remove the blower housing and other shrouds for access to engine cooling fins. Be sure all shrouds are replaced. NEVER operate an air-cooled engine without all cooling shrouds in place.

Periodically inspect any external governor or control linkage. Note if there is any binding, excessive slack or wear. If needed, lightly lubricate linkage. DO NOT alter the governor linkage in any way. Doing so may affect generator speed which may result in damage to the generator, devices connected to it or both.

Also refer to the following sections.

GENERATOR MAINTENANCE. Generators are relatively trouble-free and require little maintenance other than cleaning. Remove any debris which blocks cooling vents in generator. If available, clean, dry compressed air at less than 35 psi can be blown into generator to remove dust and debris.

Generators equipped with brushes require periodic inspection of the brushes, commutator and slip rings, depending on generator design. Removing the brushes is relatively easy on some units while partial disassembly of the generator is required on other units. Contact your dealer or refer to a service manual for manufacturer's recommended brush service procedure and to determine if professional service is needed.

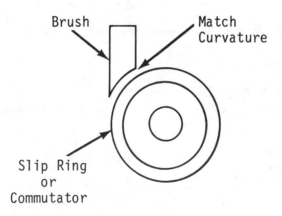

When renewing brushes be sure the correct brush is installed as similar appearing brushes may have different electrical characteristics. Always renew brushes in sets, never individually. When reinstalling a used brush be sure the curvature of the brush matches the curvature of the commutator or slip ring.

EQUIPMENT RECORDS

EQUIPMENT — Type . . . . **GENERATOR**
   Make . . . . _____
   Model . . . . _____
   Serial No. . . . . _____
   Purchase Date . . . . _____
   Dealer . . . . _____

ENGINE — Make . . . . _____
   Model . . . . _____
   Serial No. . . . . _____
   Spark Plug —
      Type . . . . _____
      Gap . . . . _____
   Oil —
      Type . . . . _____
      Viscosity . . . . _____
      Service Date . . . . _____
      Oil/Gas Mix Ratio (2 Stroke) . . . . . . _____
   Breaker Point —
      Gap . . . . _____

GENERATOR — Make . . . . _____
   Model . . . . _____
   Serial No. . . . . _____
   Fuses —
      Type, Voltage, Current Rating . . . . . _____
      Service . . . . _____

PART NUMBERS —
   Air Filter . . . . _____
   Brushes . . . . _____
   Fuel Filter . . . . _____
   Fuses . . . . _____
   Oil Filter . . . . _____
   _____ . . . . _____
   _____ . . . . _____
   _____ . . . . _____
   _____ . . . . _____
   _____ . . . . _____
   _____ . . . . _____

CHARGING 12 VOLT BATTERY. When connected to an outside 120 volt AC source, the battery charger section of the power converter will automatically keep the battery charged to the proper level. When charging, the battery will produce hydrogen which is explosive when mixed with air. Do not disconnect battery cables or produce a spark by any other means close to the battery while it is charging. Be sure to check the liquid level regularly and when adding water use distilled water to promote longer battery life. Keep battery terminals free of dirt and corrosion.

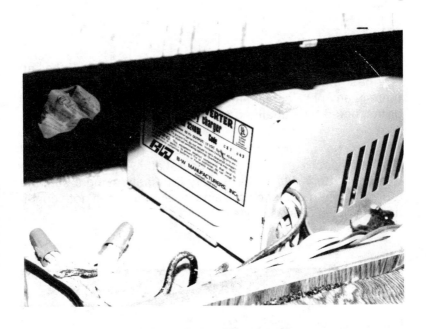

If you camp for long periods without outside 120 volt power available and unit is not equipped with an auxiliary generator, you may want to add another battery to your system. See your dealer for correct installation of the second battery **in parallel** with the first battery.

Before attempting to charge the battery, inspect the battery to determine if it is acceptable for charging. If the battery is a

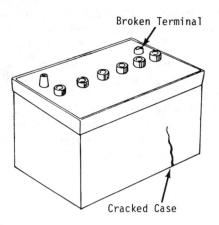

Broken Terminal

Cracked Case

"sealed" type battery DO NOT attempt to recharge it. If the battery has removable vent caps, it is probably rechargeable. If there is any physical damage the battery should be discarded or inspected by a qualified serviceman.

Clean the battery and use a solution of baking soda and water to dissolve any corrosion; do not allow cleaning solution to enter battery. Clean the battery terminals using a suitable tool so bright metal shows. Remove vent caps and note condition and level of electrolyte.

⚠DANGER

DO NOT attempt to apply a charge to a battery with frozen electrolyte. A frozen battery may explode.

If electrolyte level is low, add distilled water so the level reaches the full mark or 3/16 inch above plates. DO NOT overfill. Ask your dealer if you are unsure of the correct electrolyte level. If the battery is extremely cold, allow it to warm before filling as electrolyte level will rise as the battery warms.

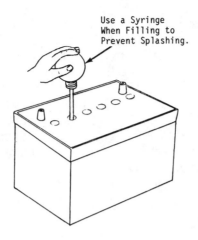

Use a Syringe When Filling to Prevent Splashing.

Place battery in a safe area as far away from the battery charger or generator set as the battery cables will reach. Connect cables to battery before turning charger ON or starting generator set. Observe polarity, positive cable from charger or generator must be connected to positive terminal of battery. Negative cable from charger must be connected to the battery negative terminal. Attach cable ends securely so there is no possibility of sparking.

⚠WARNING

DO NOT connect, disconnect or move cable ends while charging because sparking (and explosion) may result.

Chargers and generator sets vary in the rate at which the battery is charged. If the battery is a component of the generator set used to start the generator's engine, then the battery is probably charged very slowly by the generator, similar to the way the battery in an automobile is charged when the electric accessories are off. If the generator has a 12-volt DC circuit dedicated to battery charging, check the manufacturer's information for a charge rate. Fast charging occurs at a current greater than 10 amps while slow charging occurs at 10 amps and less. Fast charging will require less time to recharge a battery to a useful state of charge. But fast charging may overheat the battery, cause excessive gassing and should therefore not be used to produce a full charge. Slow charging is easier on the battery and can be used to produce full battery charge. Some generators are designed so the initial battery charge is fast but gradually tapers to a slow rate as the battery is charged. If the generator's charge rate is not known, then the battery should be monitored to prevent damage due to overheating or electrolyte boil-off.

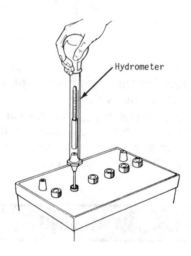

Hydrometer

Check the battery's charge at suitable intervals using a hydrometer. If a fast charge is used the battery should be checked more frequently to prevent overcharging. Consult a service manual for proper use of a hydrometer.

DO NOT OVERCHARGE the battery. Overcharging causes overheating and excessive gassing which eventually results in internal battery damage. Overcharging at a slow rate (including trickle chargers of less than one amp) over a period of time will also damage a battery.

If a battery must be maintained at full charge, such as for a standby generator, a trickle charger with an automatic shutoff should be used.

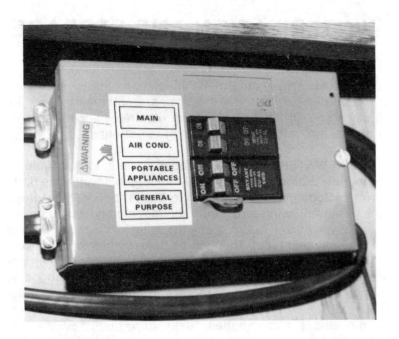

CIRCUIT BREAKERS AND FUSES. Don't replace circuit breakers or fuses with those of higher current rating than those originally installed. "Over-fusing" may cause the circuit wires to get hot and start a fire.

Most home type electrical heaters or large electrical broilers are not suitable for RV use due to excessive power requirements.

WINTERIZATION AND STORAGE

GENERAL. You should make special preparations for storing your unit in winter. All systems, components and appliances should be inspected and repaired prior to storage. Winterize the unit before removing the batteries.

FRESH WATER SYSTEM. The fresh water system should be completely drained by opening all faucets and water line drain valves including those on the water heater and water storage tank. The following procedure is recommended: Open all faucets, valves and drains. Lock the toilet valve open (if of the mechanical seal type). This can be done by blocking the seal in the bottom of the bowl open with some object of the proper size being careful it does not fall through into the holding tank. If a water filter is installed, remove filter cartridge and drain lower portion of the housing. Turn water pump on and allow to run about two minutes, then turn pump switch off. Close all faucets, drains and valves, including toilet valve. Pour appoximately six gallons of approved, non-toxic RV anti-freeze into the fresh water storage tank. Turn water pump on and briefly open each faucet. Turn the faucets off when anti-freeze flows out. Operate toilet until anti-freeze is present in the bowl. Turn the water pump off. Leave all faucets closed during storage.

⚠CAUTION

RV anti-freeze is available at your RV dealer. DO NOT use automotive type anti-freeze in the fresh water system.

Be sure to sanitize the water system as outlined on page 30 before using the RV after removing from storage. Check all components of the fresh water system for proper operation and for leaks.

DRAINAGE SYSTEM. The entire drainage system should be thoroughly drained and flushed with fresh water as follows:

Completely drain holding tanks of waste material. Flush sinks, shower and lavatory with solution of hot water, water softener and soap. Rinse well and allow solution to drain into holding tanks. Flush with clean hot water. Agitate water in holding tanks by rocking the RV, or drive vehicle a few miles. Drain holding tanks, flush with clean water and drain again. Fill traps and partially fill tanks with an anti-freeze approved for use in plastic pipes. Normally two cups of anti-freeze poured into each drain will fill the traps. Do not use anti-freeze solutions with an alcohol base.

LP-GAS SYSTEM. Cover externally mounted LP-GAS regulator to keep moisture out of the vent. Close the LP-Gas service valves on tanks. Light a range burner to consume any gas remaining in the lines. When flame burns out, turn range burner off. LP-Gas tanks should be anhydrous methanol added by an LP supplier and tanks should be refilled to correct capacity.

When removing from storage use a soapy solution to check for LP-Gas leaks. Temperature variation and vibration will cause fittings to loosen and leak.

APPLIANCES. Refrigerator should be cleaned and the door propped open. Cover exterior panels and roof vents.

Furnace should be cleaned and exterior vents covered.

Range/Oven should be cleaned, inside damper closed and range hood vent should be covered on the outside of unit.

Roof air conditioner filters should be cleaned or renewed and installed and the shroud should be covered on the outside of the unit.

BATTERIES. Recharge batteries and add water as required. Disconnect cables and store batteries in a cool, dry place. Check regularly and recharge as needed.

⚠CAUTION

DO NOT store batteries where they might be exposed to extreme heat or sparks.

INTERIOR. Drawing drapes will reduce fading of rugs and upholstery. However, if drapes and curtains have been removed for cleaning, windows should be masked with newspaper or similar material. Countertops and cabinets should be cleaned.

Leaving an air freshener agent will minimize odors from plastics and other materials. Slight opening of windows and vents will allow air circulation without worry of water entering.

NOTE

If windows and vents are left "cracked open" for ventilation, make certain light snow does not blow in and cause interior damage.

EXTERIOR. Exterior of the RV should be cleaned and liquid waxed. Locks and hinges should be oiled. It is advisable to go over all roof seams and vent flashing seams with a good roof coating material. Spraying silicone on folding antenna mechanisms will minimize effects of corrosion.

On camping trailers, canvas should be removed and stored in a dry place during winter months for added protection against mildew. If the canvas is not removed, the trailer should be set up each four to six weeks to air out and to allow canvas to dry and release any moisture that may have accumulated. Apply light coat of lubricant to exposed cables, pulleys and slides.

On all RVs, covering wheels with black plastic or canvas will eliminate direct rays of the sun on tires and will reduce the sidewall cracking.

ENGINE AND DRIVE SYSTEM STORAGE. Proper storage procedures can extend the life of equipment, especially powered equipment, by preventing damage when not being used. Exact procedures for storing will depend upon which is the off season, length of storage and the specific type of equipment. The procedure for entering the engine and drive system into storage must be coordinated with similar steps for removing the equipment from storage and with a regular maintenance program for most satisfactory results. The following outline lists some procedures applicable for extended storage of most powered equipment.

Entering Into Storage

Service engine cooling system with antifreeze. Do not attempt to drain water in an effort to prevent freezing. The heater, oil cooler, engine block and similar components may trap water which can freeze and result in extensive damage. A good quality antifreeze will also provide protection against rust and corrosion damage to the complete cooling system. Run engine until normal operating temperature is attained. Operate cab heater and all other cooling system components to circulate the antifreeze throughout system.

Drain old oil from all regularly serviced compartments such as engine crankcase, gear boxes, chain cases, etc., while oil is warm. Refill with new approved oil to the level recommended by the manufacturer.

Clean and dry all exterior surfaces. Remove all accumulated dirt and repair any damaged surfaces. Paint exposed surfaces to prevent rust.

Clean all cooling air passages and straighten, repair or renew any part which would interfere with normal flow of air. On engine cooling systems, be sure radiator and grilles are clean. On air cooled engine colling systems, remove shrouds and deflectors necessary to inspect and clean all cooling air passages. Clean all grease, oil, dirt, leaves, etc., from all cooling system components.

Lubricate all normally serviced surfaces with approved oil or grease. If equipped with grease fittings attempt to purge old grease from joint.

Inspect for worn or broken parts. Make necessary adjustments and repair all damage. Attach a description of wear and damage which is not fixed, then list all parts which have been ordered. Tighten all loose hardware.

Fuel should be either drained or treated with an approved stabilizer. On gasoline engines, all fuel should be drained from tank, filters, lines, pumps and carburetor unless specifically discouraged by manufacturer.

NOTE

Do not add fuel stabilizer to any fuel containing alcohol. Drain all fuel from tank, filter, pump, carburetor and lines before storage. Fuel containing alcohol will separate if permitted to sit for long and internal parts will be extensively damaged by corrosion.

Some manufacturers recommend coating inside of fuel tank with a small amount of oil to deter rusting in tank. Diesel fuel systems should remain filled, but most manufacturers recommend using an approved stabilizer mixed with the fuel in the tank. Filters should be serviced initially and water traps should be serviced regularly even while in storage.

Inspect and note condition of drive belts. If condition is questionable, a new belt should be installed, preferably when removing equipment from storage.

Install new filter elements. Some filters can be cleaned and serviced, but most should be installed new at this time.

Pour a small amount (usually 1 tablespoon) of oil into each cylinder of engine through hole for diesel engine injector or hole for spark plug on non-diesel engines. Crank engine with starter about 12 revolutions to distribute oil, then install spark plugs or injectors. Reconnect diesel fuel lines and spark plug wires.

Install protective caps at ends of all disconnected lines.

Seal openings of exhaust, air intake, engine dipstick and crankcase breather tube.

Remove battery or batteries and store in cool dry place. Do not permit battery to freeze and maintain fully charged, checking approximately every 30 days.

Block suspension to remove all weight from tires and suspension components. If unit is stored outside, it is best if wheels and tires can be removed and stored in cool, dark, dry location away from operating electrical equipment. Some suggest removing some air from removed tires while storing.

If necessary to store outside, use a cover to prevent entrance of water, but don't seal tightly. Sealing may cause condensation and accelerate rusting. Caulking is especially susceptible to deterioration during storage.

Removing From Storage
Remove protective covering from around equipment. Check for obvious damage to covering and equipment.

Install tires and wheels. Service tires and inflated suspension components with correct amount of air. Remove any blocks used during storage.

Charge, then install battery making sure that it is properly retained. Clean cables and battery posts, then attach cables to correct terminals.

Remove covers from exhaust, air intake and crankcase breather tube.

Remove any protective caps from lines disconnected during disassembly. Be sure ends are clean, then reconnect lines.

Check all filters. Install new filter, clean or service as required.

Adjust all drive belts to correct tension as recommended by manufacturer. New belts should be installed if condition is questionable.

Fill fuel tank with correct type of fuel. Check for leaks. Gaskets may dry up or carburetor needle valve may stick during storage. Repair any problems before attempting to start. Drain water traps and check condition of fuel filters. Bleed diesel fuel system following procedure outlined by manufacturer before attempting to start.

Check for worn or broken parts and repair before returning to service.

Lubricate all surfaces normally lubricated with oil or grease.

Check all vents and cooling passages for restrictions such as insect, bird or animal nests.

Check oil in all compartments such as engine crankcase, gear boxes, chain cases, etcs., for proper level. Evidence of too much oil may indicate water settled below oil. Drain old oil if contamination is suspected or if time of storage exceeds recommended time change interval. Fill to proper level with correct type of oil.

Fill engine cooling system to correct level. Antifreeze solutions which improve summer cooling ability as well as providing rust and corrosion protection should be used. Check for leak if much fluid has leaked from system during storage.

CARE AND MAINTENANCE

BODY AND SUSPENSION SYSTEM. Life of exterior paint can be extended by maintaining it in a waxed condition. This not only preserves the paint, but allows for easier removal of dirt and road tars. Use of touch-up paint from small areas keeps the RV in like-new condition. To keep it clean, simply hose it down with water, wiping the wet surface with a cloth or sponge, if necessary. Never wipe the metal surface when it is dry. Do not use harsh abrasives or strong solvents on exterior surfaces. Accumulated dirt or road film should loosen easily with warm water and a mild detergent. Rinse with plain water. When dry, apply a coat of good quality automotive wax to protect the finish.

In areas where heavy salt spray is evident, use of clear acrylic spray on the "A" frame, wheels and hitch assembly will help control corrosive effects of salt.

The leaf spring suspension system requires no lubrication. To reduce corrosive effects, lubricant/preservatives are available which can be sprayed on axles, U-bolts, springs, etc., periodically.

Moving parts of windows and latches should be kept adjusted and maintained. It is advisable to lubricate the windows with a light oil or powdered graphite at least once a year. Screens may be cleaned by gently wiping with a damp cloth or soft flat brush designed for the purpose.

Cleaning of the canvas on camping trailers is very important. Foreign matter, such as tree sap, bird droppings, etc., coming in contact with the exterior surface of the canvas can adversely affect the water repellancy of the canvas. In some cases, this may also start rotting or decaying of canvas. Canvas may be cleaned by the following methods:

1. Rinse the canvas thoroughly with cool water and allow to dry completely.

2. Brush with a dry sponge or soft bristle brush while dry or after wetting and rinse with cool water.

3. A "Dry Kleen" pad can be used to erase most types of marks and dirt off dry canvas. "Dry Kleen" pads are available at RV dealers.

Sprays are available for renewing the water repellancy of the canvas.

⚠CAUTION

Canvas should never be stored wet for extended periods of time because it may mildew. If canvas must be stored wet, set camping trailer up as soon as possible and allow it to dry.

INTERIOR AND APPLIANCES. The interior of your RV may be any of several finishes and textures. Never use strong detergents or abrasive cleaners on walls or ceilings. Most surfaces will clean with a soft cloth which has been dampened with mild liquid detergent in warm water. Always avoid the use of large amounts of water. Many panel suppliers suggest that one of the aerosol products designed for cleaning and preserving wood surfaces may be excellent if used in accordance with manufacturers instructions.

Allow the range top to cool, then clean it with hot soapy water. Use a damp cloth to clean chrome surfaces. Grease splatters, which may bake onto the surfaces, should be wiped off before they have time to harden. Use a toothpick to clean clogged burner ports. Clean the oven with a commercial cleaner after each trip, or as necessary. DO NOT apply cleaner to aluminum gas tubing, thermostat sensing bulb or electrical components.

To clean the range hood and power vent, first remove the plastic light cover and wash it in mild detergent and water. Remove the filter and run hot, soapy water over it until grease is dissolved. Allow filter to drain dry, then reinstall it with arrows pointing in toward housing. Clean housing, fan and motor surfaces frequently to remove grease. The chrome trim should be cleaned with a good glass cleaner or with warm water and a soft cloth.

Remove food and ice from refrigerator after each trip. Clean interior with warm water and liquid dish soap. Wipe dry with a soft dry cloth. DO NOT use abrasive cleaning material as it will scratch interior surfaces. Prop door open during periods of nonuse.

Remove and clean the roof air conditioner filter at least once every two weeks if it is used extensively. Wash filter with soap and water. Do not operate the air conditioner for extended periods without a filter.

PLUMBING AND FIXTURES. Sinks, baths, showers or other fiberglass fixtures should be cleaned only with warm water and mild detergent or special cleaners. Harsh abrasives may scratch or discolor the surfaces. It is recommended that NO ammonia or any cleaner with ammonia in it, be used on fiberglass.

The toilet requires little or no maintenance. An occasional spraying of the bowl sealing blade with silicone spray will retain the original smooth operating condition. When cleaning the bowl, use an approved non-abrasive cleaner. Do not use common household cleaners which have a high acid content as they may damage rubber seals. Refer to the recommendations from the toilet or holding tank manufacturers relating to chemical additives which may be appropriate for those components.

Plumbing system drains should be kept clean. Chemical products recommended for plastic pipe may be used in the drain lines.

CONDENSATION AND VENTILATION. Moisture condensing on windows is a visible sign that there is too much moisture inside the RV. This excessively high humidity can cause mildew, staining and rotting of woodwork or paneling.

Humidity should be controlled to the point where little or no condensation appears on the inside surface of the glass. The best way to reduce moisture inside the RV is to bring in fresh outside air through ventilation. Use the exhaust and vent fans to ventilate the inside to minimize moisture build up when cooking, bathing or washing. Air out the vehicle to reduce humidity by opening doors, windows and ceiling vents several times a day.

FIRE SAFETY. To continue the excellent record for fire safety exhibited among recreational vehicle owners, it is recommended that you follow these safety suggestions:

Establish good housekeeping practices. Do not allow combustible materials to accumulate. Be sure that flammable liquids are stored in approved containers in a well ventilated space.

Provide readily accessible fire extinguishers.

Avoid the use of flammable solvents or products containing these solvents within the RV unit.

Install smoke detectors following the smoke detector manufacturers installation instructions. These detectors provide early warning in the event of a fire.

Do not smoke in bed. Do not overload electrical wiring. Do not leave food cooking unattended. Do not permit children to play with the controls of LP-Gas or electrical appliances. Do not use matches or other open flame to check for LP-Gas leaks.

Do make all members of your party aware of all exits (including escape windows and hatches).

If a fire does start, get all members of your party outside. If it is a small fire, use the fire extinguisher. If the fire cannot be extinguished quickly, get out of the RV. Close the LP-Gas service valves on tanks, if possible. Call the fire department and stay a safe distance from the vehicle. Do not re-enter the RV until officials declare it safe to do so.

WHEELS AND BRAKES. Wheel bearings should be cleaned and packed in accordance with the RV manufacturers instructions. This may vary from approximately every 2000 miles on some camping and travel trailers to as much as 30,000 miles on some motorhomes.

Electric brakes should be checked periodically to determine condition of magnets and drums and whether wiring connections are still secure. Brakes can be adjusted with a conventional brake adjusting tool. Brakes should be adjusted to activate ahead of the tow vehicle brakes for best road control.

Wheel lug bolts or nuts should be checked for tightness before starting on a trip and periodically thereafter.

Check tire air pressure while tires are cool. Heat generated by surface friction will increase the tire air pressure approximately 6 to 9 psi. Do not bleed air out of a hot tire.

SPARK PLUGS. The gasoline engines, used to power recreational vehicles, generator sets and most other powered equipment, all use a spark plug to ignite the combustible mixture. If the spark plug doesn't deliver a spark, the engine won't run. Of course other parts of the ignition system can also cause problems, but since the spark plug operates in such a hostile environment, it is most often the cause of not starting or poor running.

At least once each year the ignition systems should be included in a "tune up" to provide efficient engine operation and lessen the possibility of a breakdown. Depending on the complexity of the tune-up procedure, the tune-up may require a professional mechanic or may be performed by someone with the required mechanical expertise. Tune-up specifications are available in service and maintenance manuals or often from the operator's manual for the specific equipment.

The most frequent problem is spark plug fouling due to an accumulation of oil and fuel on the spark plug electrodes. When an engine begins to miss or is difficult to start, the first item to check is the spark plugs (presuming it is not out of gas).

Identification

Spark plugs are manufactured in a variety of sizes, shapes and specifications to conform to different engine designs and applications. The large variety of available plugs also makes it easy to install the WRONG spark plug, which can result in serious engine damage.

Each spark plug manufacturer has a unique code to identify the characteristics of its spark plugs, and application charts are available from the manufacturers and distributors.

THREAD SIZE. The end of the spark plug that screws into the cylinder head is threaded. The diameter indicates the thread size — 10mm, 14mm, 18mm, ⅞-mm, etc. *Thread pitch* is an established industry standard but it may be indicated differently, as in "½-inch pipe."

SEALING TYPE. If a special sealing washer is used to seal between the spark plug and cylinder head, the surface of the head and plug must both be flat. Another method of sealing is with a carefully controlled angled (tapered) seat on the spark plug and a matching seat machined into the cylinder head. Never attempt to install a spark plug with the incorrect type of sealing.

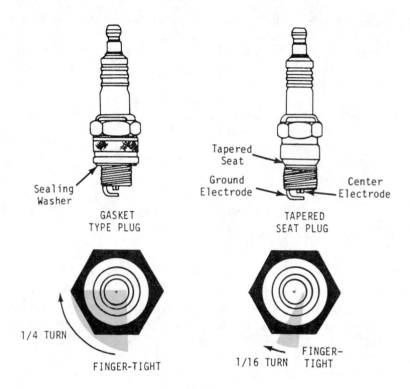

GASKET
TYPE PLUG

Sealing
Washer

Tapered
Seat

Ground
Electrode

TAPERED
SEAT PLUG

Center
Electrode

1/4 TURN

FINGER-TIGHT

1/16 TURN

FINGER-
TIGHT

TIGHTENING WITH
SOCKET WRENCH

A sealing washer is used only when the surface of the cylinder head and the spark plug are both flat (left). A cylinder head with a tapered seat requires a spark plug with a carefully controlled angled seat (right) that matches the angle machined into the cylinder head.

REACH. The length of the threaded section measured from the gasket or tapered seat to the combustion chamber end of the thread is the *reach dimension.* Some standard reaches are ⅜-inch, 7/16-inch, 0.492-inch, ½-inch and ¾-inch; however, spark plugs with different reaches are available. An engine can be damaged by a spark plug with the wrong reach even if the reach is very close.

Spark plugs with various reaches are available. Small engines usually are equipped with a ⅜-inch reach spark plug. Circled electrodes illustrate the difference between plugs normally used in two-stroke cycle engines (left) and 4 stroke engines.

HEAT RANGE. Heat generated during combustion is transferred from the center electrode and insulator to the plug shell, then to the cylinder head and finally to the engine-cooling air or liquid coolant.

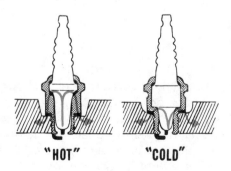

"HOT"   "COLD"

Temperature of the spark plug tip is controlled by the distance the heat must travel to reach the cooling surface of the engine's cylinder head. Heat range codes are unique to each spark plug manufacturer and cannot be compared.

Spark plug temperature is important to engine operaion. If the spark plug surface is TOO HOT, the fuel-air mixture may be ignited before a spark occurs (pre-ignition). If the spark plug surface is TOO COLD, the plug will foul with unburned or partially burned combustion products. Some manufacturers identify the spark plug heat ranges by a range of numbers. Be careful, however, because the numbers indicating cold to hot range may run from small to large *or* from large to small. The heat range codes are unique to each spark plug manufacturer and cannot be compared directly with plugs from another.

SPECIAL FEATURES. Engine design and application to specific equipment will usually require that the spark plug incorporate some special features. Some of the features may include electrode shape or material, non-standard hex size and special radio interference protection. The equipment manufacturer considers each special feature of the recommended spark plug to be necessary, and installing plugs with different features is discouraged.

SELECTION. Check the appropriate engine service manual, operators book or spark plug application chart to find the specific spark plug the manufacturer recommends. If the removed spark plug is different from the recommended one, find out why. Slight differences in heat range may be desirable because of operating conditions, as for lighter-than-normal load or constant overload.

Removing And Installing Spark Plugs

The engine should be allowed to cool before removing spark plugs. Pull the wire connector from the spark plug, being careful not to damage the wire or connector. Grip the boot at the connector and twist until loosened, then pull connector away from spark plug. Some spark plugs may be hard to reach, but do not pull on the wire. Grip and pull only on the connector boot. Be careful not to slip and injure yourself when connector releases from spark plug.

Use the correct size of spark plug wrench to turn the spark plug counter-clockwise approximately 1 turn. Apply steady

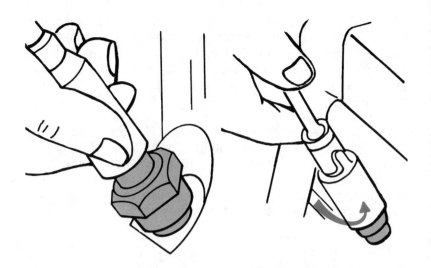

pressure to wrench until plug loosens. Use penetrating oil if plug is difficult to remove. Forcing a spark plug that is seized will nearly always damage threads in cylinder head.

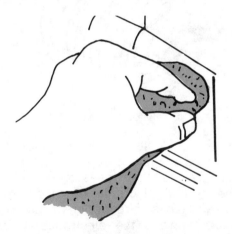

Remove wrench, then clean spark plug and pocket around plug. It is important to remove all of the dirt which could either fall into engine cylinder or onto sealing surface for spark plug. Clean the area with a brush and by blowing with compressed air. Remove the spark plug completely, then use a cloth to clean the threaded opening for spark plug. Be sure that gasket is removed with plug, if so equipped.

If spark plug is difficult to remove by hand, after loosening, carbon may have built up in threaded area of cylinder head. Inspect the threads carefully and clean using a thread-chaser tool before installing a new plug. If spark plug has seized or threads are damaged, repair damage before installing new spark plug.

Check the appropriate engine service manual, operator's book, spark plug application chart or parts supplier to find the type of spark plug recommended by the manufacturer. If the removed spark plug is different than the one recommended, find out why. All spark plugs are not alike and installation of the wrong plug can damage the engine.

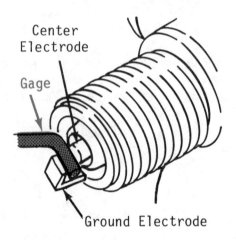

Center Electrode

Gage

Ground Electrode

Inspect the new spark plug for correct electrode gap. Check the engine service manual or operator's book for recommended electrode gap, then measure gap between center electrode and ground electrode by inserting the correct thickness of gage. Gap is correct when the gage drags slightly as it is pulled between the electrodes. Change gap, if necessary, by bending the ground electrode slightly. If the gap is nearly zero, check to be sure that the plug has not been dropped and damaged.

Install the spark plug by hand into the threaded hole until snug, then use a wrench to finish tightening. Check the engine service manual for recommended torque. Spark plugs with

new gaskets should usually be tightened ¼ turn after seating by hand. Spark plugs with tapered seat (no gasket) should usually be tightened 1/16 turn after seating by hand. Do not overtighten as the threads in the engine can be damaged.

Special Notes

Damaged threads in cylinder head are usually caused by improper spark plug installation. Aluminum cylinder heads are more easily damaged than cast iron and therefore more care should be exercised when installing plugs in aluminum. The following precautions should always be observed, especially when servicing spark plugs which are installed in aluminum cylinder heads.

1. Always cool engine before removing or installing spark plugs. Because of the different expansion rate, the threads of the spark plug and the threads in the cylinder head are distorted when Hot. The expansion of aluminum cylinder heads is much different than steel spark plugs.

2. Remove and inspect any spark plug which is difficult to install. Be careful not to cross thread spark plug, especially into the soft threads of an aluminum cylinder head. Inspect spark plug for bent or damaged threads. Use a thread-chaser tool to clean threads in cylinder head.

3. Use caution when removing spark plug that is difficult to turn. First, be sure that engine has completely cooled. Use penetrating oil and work cautiously, first loosening, then tightening small amounts until spark plug is removed. Finally, be prepared to accomplish the machining necessary to repair the destroyed threads in the cylinder head.
4. Tighten spark plugs to the recommended torque. Overtightening a steel spark plug in an aluminum cylinder head will easily distort and damage the softer aluminum threads. Insufficient tightening may permit burning gasses to escape past the threads and sealing surface which can also easily destroy the cylinder head threads.
5. Some manufacturers recommend the use of anti-seize compound on threads of spark plugs used in aluminum cylinder heads.
6. Make sure that correct spark plug is installed. Plug with incorrect thread length may protrude past threads in cylinder head permitting carbon to accumulate on spark plug threads. Subsequent removal of spark plug will require carbon coated threads of plug to pass through and damage the threads in cylinder head.

Servicing Plugs

The appearance of a spark plug will be altered by use, and an examination of the plug tip can contribute useful information which may assist in obtaining better spark plug life. It must be remembered that the contributing factors differ in 2 stroke and 4 stroke engine operation and although the appearance of two spark plugs may be similar, the corrective measures may depend on whether the engine is of 2 stroke or 4 stroke design.

Normal plug appearance in 4 stroke cycle engine. Insulator is light tan to gray in color and electrodes are not burned. Renew plug at regular intervals as recommended by engine manufacturer.

Appearance of 4 stroke cycle spark plug indicating wet fouling; a wet, black oily film is over entire firing end of plug. Cause may be oil getting by worn valve guides, worn oil rings or plugged breather or breather valve in tappet chamber.

Appearance of 4 stroke cycle spark plug indicating cold fouling. Cause of cold fouling may be use of a too-cold plug, excessive idling or light loads, carburetor choke out of adjustment, defective spark plug wire or boot, carburetor adjusted too "rich" or low engine compression.

Appearance of 4 stroke cycle spark plug indicating over-heating. Check for plugged cooling fins, bent or damaged blower housing, engine being operated without all shields in place or other causes of engine over-heating. Also can be caused by too lean a fuel-air mixture of spark plug not tightened properly.

Normal appearance of plug removed from a 2 stroke cycle engine. Insulator is light tan to gray in color, few deposits are present and electrodes not burned.

Appearance of plug from 2 stroke cycle engine indicating wet fouling. A damp or wet black carbon coating is formed over entire firing end. Could be caused by a too-cold plug, excessive idling, improper fuel-lubricating oil mixture or carburetor adjustment too rich.

Appearance of plug from 2 stroke cycle engine indicating overheating. Insulator has gray or white blistered appearance and electrodes may be burned. Could be caused by use of a too-hot plug, carburetor adjustment too lean, "sticky" piston rings, engine overloaded, or cooling fins plugged causing engine to run too hot.

Spark plugs can sometimes be cleaned, but the easiest and best way of assuring the best possible condition is to install a new spark plug of correct type.

Spark plug electrode gap can be changed by bending the ground electrode. Refer to manufacturer's specifications for desired clearance between the center electrode and the side (ground) electrode. Faces of electrodes should be parallel. Special tools are available for measuring the gap and bending the ground electrode.

ENGINE OIL. Engines are lubricated using a variety of methods; however, all must be lubricated. Check with a local dealer for explanation of what happens when an operator **doesn't make sure** that the engine has enough oil.

Some 2 stroke engines used to power boats and other recreational equipment are lubricated by mixing oil with the gasoline. The engine doesn't check to see if your intentions were pure. If the wrong type or wrong amount of oil is used, the engine will let you know that it wasn't and repair is sure to cost more than the oil.

Attempts to operate any engine with little or no oil is sure to result in damage to the engine. Operating with even a slightly reduced amount of oil will overheat the remaining oil very quickly. The excessive heat will reduce the lubricating quality of the oil, which in turn increases friction causing even more heat to be absorbed by the oil. The spiral often ends with dramatic damage to the engine, but serious damage has probably occurred even if unnoticed.

Engine damage can result from lack of proper lubrication, caused by overheating even **with** the recommended amount of oil. High oil temperature may be caused by the engine overheating from not enough coolant, blocked cooling air passages or a variety of other problems which could have been prevented by proper owner maintenance.

Heavy loads including trailer pulling will increase engine heat and subsequently will result in higher oil temperature. Many late model engines already operate at high temperature to assist emission control and to improve fuel mileage and additional heat may cause serious damage. Installation, of Trailer pulling packages, which include increased oil capacity and/or oil coolers, is recommended if not included in standard design.

SELECTING RIGHT TYPE OF OIL. Early in the development of modern gasoline and diesel engines, it was obvious that certain qualities in the lubricating oil would increase engine life. In 1911 the SAE established guidelines for grading engine oil viscosity and in 1947 the API adopted a classification system that divided oils into three groups to indicate •straight mineral oils, •those containing oxidation inhibitors and •heavy-duty oil, which included oxidation inhibitors and detergent-dispersant additives. These early grades and classifications are still being refined and expanded to meet the demands of modern engines.

Each container of oil is marked with the SAE and API service classification so that people servicing and operating equipment can easily select an oil that meets the needs of the engine as determined by the manufacturer.

SAE viscosity grades indicate the resistance to flow at specific temperatures. Standard numbers (5W, 10W, 20W, 20, 30, 40 and 50) range from very thin oil suitable for engine operation in very low temperatures to thicker oils suitable for higher temperatures. Multiviscosity oils are those that test within the range of one of the W grades at −18°C and also within the range of non-W grade when tested at 100°C.

Select an oil viscosity suitable for the ambient temperature. In summer, consider the highest ambient temperature; in winter, consider the lowest expected temperature. In winter, the oil must be thin enough to permit easy starting. Check the engine or equipment operator's book for the SAE viscosity grades the manufacturer recommends.

The API classifications describe the type of service and coincide with ASTM-established test methods that help engine manufacturers determine which oil should be used. The chart explains the current API classification letter designation codes.

Letter Designation	API Engine Service Description

Formerly for Utility Gasoline and Diesel Engine Service

SA Service typical of older engines operated under such mild conditions that the protection afforded by compounded oils is not required. This category has no performance requirements and oils in this category should not be used in any engine unless specifically recommended by the equipment manufacturer.

Minumum-Duty Gasoline Engine Service

SB Service typical of older gasoline engines operated under such mild conditions that only minimum protection afforded by compounding is desired. Oils designed for this service have been used since the 1930s and provide only antiscuff capability and resistance to oil oxidation and bearing corrosion. Oils in this category should not be used in any engine unless specifically recommended by the equipment manufacturer.

1964 Gasoline Engine Warranty Service

SC Service typical of gasoline engines in 1964-1967 models of passenger cars and trucks operating under engine manufacturers' warranties in effect during those model years. Oil designed for this service provide control of high- and low-temperature deposits, wear, rust and corrosion in gasoline engines.

1968 Gasoline Engine Warranty Maintenance Service

SD Service typical of gasoline engines in 1968 through 1970 models of passenger cars and some trucks operating under engine manufacturers'

Letter Designation	API Engine Service Description

SD Cont.

SD warranties in effect during those model years. Also may apply to certain 1971 and/or later models, as specified (or recommended) in the operator's book. Oils designed for this service provide more protection than Category SC oils against high- and low-temperature engine deposits, wear, rust and corrosion in gasoline engines. API Engine Service Category SD oil may be used when API Engine Service Category SC is recommended.

1972 Gasoline Engine Warranty Maintenance Service

SE Service typical of gasoline engines in passenger cars and some trucks beginning with 1972 and certain 1971 models operating under engine manufacturers' warranties. Oils designed for this service provide more protection than Category SD oils against oil oxidation, high-temperature engine deposits, rust and corrosion in gasoline engines. API Engine Service Category SE oil may be used when either Category SC or SD is recommended.

1980 Gasoline Engine Warranty Maintenance Service

SF Service typical of gasoline engines in passenger cars and some trucks beginning with the 1980 model operating under engine manufacturers' recommended maintenance procedures. Oils developed for this service provide increased oxidation stability and improved anti-wear performance over Category SE oils. These oils also provide protection against engine deposits, rust and corrosion. Oils meeting API Service Category SF may be used when Category SC, SD or SE oil is recommended.

Letter Designation	API Engine Service Description

Light-Duty Diesel Engine Service

CA for Diesel Engine Service

Service typical of diesel engines operated in mild to moderate duty with high-quality fuels. Oils designed for this service provide protection from bearing corrosion and from ring belt deposits in some naturally aspirated diesel engines when using fuels of such quality that they impose no unusual requirements for wear and deposit protection. Widely used in the late 1940s and 1950s but should not be used in any engine unless specifically recommended by the equipment manufacturer.

Moderate Duty Diesel Engine Service

CB for Diesel Engine Service

Service typical of diesel engines operated in mild to moderate duty, but with lower quality fuels that necessitate more protection from wear and deposits. Oils designed for this service were introduced in 1949. Such oils provide necessary protection from bearing corrosion and from high-temperature deposits in normally aspirated diesel engines with higher sulfur fuels.

Moderate-Duty Diesel and Gasoline Engine Service

CC for Diesel Engine Service

Service typical of lightly supercharged diesel engines operated in moderate to severe duty and has included certain heavy-duty gasoline engines. Oils designed for this service were introduced in 1961 and used in many trucks and in industrial and construction equipment and farm tractors. These oils provide protection from high temperature deposits in lightly supercharged diesels and also from rust, corrosion and low-temperature deposits in gasoline engines.

Letter Designation	API Engine Service Description

Severe-Duty Diesel Engine Service

CD for Diesel Engine Service

Service typical of supercharged diesel engines in high-speed, high-output duty requiring highly effective control of wear and deposits. Oils designed for this service were introduced in 1955. They provide protection from bearing corrosion and from high-temperature deposits in supercharged diesel engines when using fuels of a wide quality range.

Early classifications ML, MM and MS are approximately like the later designations SA, SB and SC. Most engines that specify use of oils identified with SC, SD or (early) MS designation may safely use SE or SF oils. If the manufacturer calls for SA, SB, (early) ML or (early) MM designations, the additives in other oil classifications may be harmful and should not be used.

For 2 stroke engines, check with manufacturer for recommended type. Liquid cooled engines such as outboard engines operate at cooler temperatures than air cooled 2 stroke engines. Snowmobiles operate with different considerations and oil formulated for them probably won't be right either. Many equipment manufacturers market an oil to reduce confusion and to make sure that people who use their products can know which oil is OK.

MIXING GASOLINE AND OIL FOR TWO STROKE ENGINES.
Two stroke engines used for chain saws, string trimmers and other powered equipment are lubricated by oil mixed with the gasoline. The manufacturers carefully determine which type of oil and how much oil should be mixed with gasoline to provide the most desirable operation, then list these mixing instructions in the operator's manual. Often two or more oil to gasoline ratios will be listed depending upon type of oil or severity of service. It is important to always follow the recommended mixing instructions, because mixing the wrong amount of oil or using the wrong type of oil can cause exten-

sive engine damage. Too much oil can cause lower power, spark plug fouling and excessive carbon build up. Not enough oil will cause inadequate lubrication and will probably result in scuffing, seizure and other forms of damage.

⚠CAUTION

It is important to mix oil with gasoline for proper lubrication of 2 stroke engines designed for this type of lubrication; but, engines designed for operation with gasoline only will not operate properly if oil is mixed with the fuel. Be sure of manufacturer's fuel recommendation and fill tank ONLY with that type of fuel or mix. Storage tank should be marked to indicate if it contains gasoline and oil mix or gasoline only.

Some manufacturers recommend only regular gasoline and caution not to use low-lead, unleaded, premium gasoline, gasohol or other blends of gasoline, while other manufacturers may recommend using only low-lead gasoline. Follow the suggestions of the equipment manufacturer. NEVER use gasoline which has been stored for a long time or fluid which may not be gasoline.

Accurate measurement of gasoline and oil is necessary to assure correct lubrication. Proper quantities of gasoline and oil for some of the more common mix ratios are listed below.

Ratio	Gasoline	Oil
10:1	.63 Gallon	½ Pint (237mL)
14:1	.88 Gallon	½ Pint (237mL)
16:1	1.00 Gallon	½ Pint (237mL)
20:1	1.25 Gallons	½ Pint (237mL)
30:1	1.88 Gallons	½ Pint (237mL)
32:1	2.00 Gallons	½ Pint (237mL)
50:1	3.13 Gallons	½ Pint (237mL)

Ratio	Gasoline	Oil
10:1	1 Gallon	.79 Pint (379mL)
14:1	1 Gallon	.57 Pint (270mL)
16:1	1 Gallon	.50 Pint (237mL)
20:1	1 Gallon	.40 Pint (189mL)
30:1	1 Gallon	.27 Pint (126mL)
32:1	1 Gallon	.25 Pint (118mL)
50:1	1 Gallon	.16 Pint (76mL)

When mixing, use a separate approved safety container which is large enough to hold the desired amount of fuel with additional space for mixing. Pour about ½ of the required amount of gasoline into container, add the required amount of gasoline into container, add the required amount of oil, then shake vigorously until completely mixed. Pour remaining amount of gasoline into container, then complete mixing by shaking. Serious engine damage can be caused by incomplete mixing. NEVER attempt to mix gasoline and oil in the equipment fuel tank.

SAFETY HINT

All fuel is potentially dangerous. If the fuel wouldn't burn, it wouldn't be used as engine fuel. Always be careful. Fire requires three things:

1. Oxygen   2. Fuel   3. Ignition

Oxygen is in the air and fuel can be wood, paper, grass, leaves, rubber, gasoline or diesel fuel. A match will ignite paper easily and just about any spark or flame can be used to ignite gasoline or diesel fuel, especially when you least suspect a fire.

Always observe the following:

Use only properly marked, approved safety containers for mixing and storing fuel. Make sure container is in good condition.

Mix fuel and oil and refuel only outdoors.

Stop engine and allow to cool before refueling.

Never smoke near equipment refueling area or where the odor of fuel is detected.

Avoid spilling fuel. Accidental spills should be cleaned completely before starting engine.

Observe safe procedures at all times.

— Use safety container for mixing and storing fuel.

— Handle gasoline and oil only in well ventilated area away from all flames, sparks and other ignition sources.

— Be careful not to spill fuel or overfill fuel tank. Wipe up any spilled fuel immediately.

— Don't fill fuel tank while engine is running.

— Leave some room for fuel to expand in the equipment fuel tank when filling. Do not fill tank to overflowing.

CHANGING FOUR STROKE ENGINE OIL. The following describes oil changing for 4 stroke engines, but the procedures are similar for gearboxes, transmissions, chain cases, etc.

Draining the old contaminated oil is a convenient way of removing a significant amount of impurities from the lubrication system. The operator's manual lists a specific length (in hours, miles, months, etc.) which the manufacturer considers an appropriate regular interval between oil changes. Oil should sometimes be changed more often if "operating in dusty conditions" or other forms of severe service. The oil change interval should be shorter for a new or freshly rebuilt engine to remove the wear particles produced during break-in.

High temperature, combustion blow-by, rich fuel mixture, high humidity, high sulphur content (of Diesel fuel), etc., all contaminate the oil. Filtering the oil extends the length of time between oil changes and filter should also be serviced at recommended intervals.

Drain the old oil from engine while engine is hot. Operate the engine at low idle for about 5 minutes before draining. Stop engine, position a pan large enough to hold all of the oil under the drain plug, then remove the oil drain plug. Be careful not to drop the hot plug into the pan. Allow enough time to allow all of the oil to drain and make sure that equipment is on level ground so all oil will drain. Clean drain plug and opening, check and install a new gasket on plug if damaged, then reinstall drain plug. Be careful not to overtighten and strip threads for drain plug.

If a renewable canister type oil filter is used, check operator's manual for recommended change interval. To remove filter, locate drain pan below filter, then turn filter counter-clockwise. The filter will contain about 1 quart of oil. Clean surface of engine around filter and make sure gasket for filter is completely removed. Pour some of the new oil into center of the new filter before installing so lubrication system will not be starved when first starting engine, coat the gasket with oil, then install the filter. Usually filters are tightened about ½ turn past snug, but be sure to check instructions printed on the carton for the new filter.

Fill the engine with the proper amount of new oil of the type recommended by the equipment manufacturer. The correct type of oil depends upon engine design, temperature and type of service. The "BEST" oil will not be the same for all applications. Check to be sure oil level is correct, then start engine. Check to be sure oil pressure quickly reaches correct pressure and that oil is not leaking. Operate engine for about 5 minutes, while checking for leaks. Stop engine and repair any leaks, then fill to correct level and recheck if any leaks were discovered. Check oil level after engine has been stopped and allowed to drain back into crankcase, about 5 minutes. Be sure oil level is exactly correct, then record when the oil (and filter) was changed so that the proper interval can be maintained.

Inspect the drained oil for any easily identifiable indications of problems. If the oil is heavily contaminated, the interval between oil and filter changes should be reduced. Dilution of the oil by water, anti-freeze or fuel is probably caused by mechanical damage which should be repaired immediately. Contamination by larger chunks of metal, gaskets, "O" rings or other identifiable engine parts should be quickly corrected.

Where Oil Can Be Tested

Some equipment distributors have their own oil analysis labs to test oil for their customers and sometimes for others. Ask local dealers about the availability of such services. Independent oil analysis laboratories are also located in the United States and Canada, and a number of them belong to the Spectrometric Oil Analysis Laboratory Association (SOALA), which provided much of the information for this article. SOALA members include:

Ana-Laboratories, Inc.
111 Harding Avenue
Bellmawr, NJ 08031

Analysts, Inc.
61 Sutton Lane
Box 181
Piscataway, NJ 08854

Chemical & Geological
Laboratories of Alaska, Inc.
Box 4-1276
Anchorage, AL 99509

Lubricon, Inc.
Box 41506
Indianapolis, IN 46241

Optimal Systems, Inc.
Box 1182
Atlanta, GA 30301

Spectro/Metrics, Inc.
(Wear Check)
35 Executive Park Drive NE
Atlanta, GA 30329

Wear Check International LTD.
29-17 Connell Court
Toronto, Ont. M8Z 5T7

BATTERY CONDITION CHECK. The state of charge and electrolyte level should be periodically checked for all batteries.

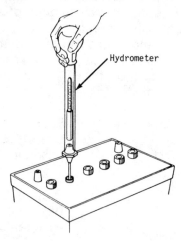

Hydrometer

Check the battery's charge using a hydrometer; consult a service manual if a description of proper use of a hydrometer is needed.

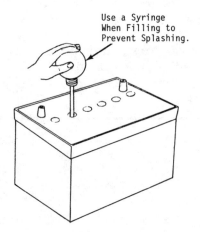

Use a Syringe When Filling to Prevent Splashing.

To check the electrolyte level, remove the vent caps and note level of fluid. If necessary, add distilled water so the electrolyte level is at full mark or 3/16 inch above plates. DO NOT overfill. Ask your dealer if you are unsure as to the correct electrolyte level for the battery.

⚠️WARNING

Batteries expel explosive hydrogen gas. Be sure area around battery is well-ventilated. DO NOT smoke or allow open flame or sources of spark in area around battery.

Battery terminals and wire leads must be clean and tight. Protective covers as well as a light coat of grease on the terminals and leads will help prevent corrosion. A neutralizing solution of baking soda and water applied to the terminals and leads will dissolve the corrosion; do not allow solution to enter battery.

To maintain a full charge in the battery, a slow charge battery charger with automatic shutoff may be used.

⚠️WARNING

Batteries contain highly corrosive acid which can spill out if the battery is overturned or the battery case is broken. Protective clothing and eyewear is recommended when handling or servicing batteries. IMMEDIATELY flush with water any area contacting battery fluid then obtain medical aid.

V-BELTS. V-Belts may be the item most overlooked during maintenance, but proper care and maintenance of V-belts and their sheaves (pulleys) can yield great rewards. The nature of V-belts makes preventive maintenance relatively easy. Unlike fatigue or flaws in direct drives that are very often invisible until an abrupt failure, V-belts and sheaves wear gradually and usually give advance warning of failure. Nonetheless, it is important to recognize the warnings.

Before attempting any maintenance, be sure the controlling switch is in the OFF position and lock it in OFF if possible. Other safety procedures — such as blocking — may be required to assure safety.

All belts and sheaves will wear as part of their life's cycle. As wear occurs, the belts will ride lower in the grooves; because the sheave center distance must be increased to compensate, a worn belt is, in effect, longer than a new one.

V-belts grip by wedging in the pulley grooves. Belts that are too loose cause slippage, loss of power, loss of speed and rapid wear to both the belt and the sheave. A howl or squeal indicates that the belt is too loose or the load is too heavy.

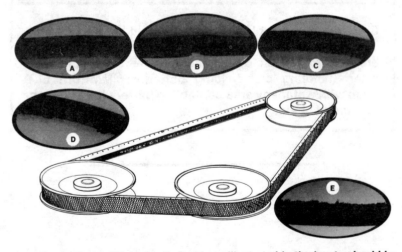

Visually check condition of belt. Problems illustrated in the insets should be corrected and new belt installed. Inset "A" shows cracks or cuts in belt. Inset "B" shows localized burned section of belt caused by drive pulley turning with belt not moving. Inset "C" shows frayed and worn friction sides. Inset "D" shows notched belt with sections broken loose or out. Inset "E" shows frayed and worn backside of belt which is usually caused by incorrectly adjusted belt guard.

ALIGNMENT AND TENSION OF V-BELTS. Check to be sure sheaves are properly aligned because misalignment can cause excessive wear to the belt sidewall. Unusual wear of the belt outer cover is an indication of more serious mechanical trouble. Belts engineered to operate without the cover, such as cut or raw-edge belts, will become narrow as they wear. This wear decreases belt tension and may cause the belt to slip.

Belts that are too tight will wear rapidly and the excessive side loads may damage drive shafts and bushings (or bearings).

Inspect the drive elements when you remove belts. Relieve belt tension by loosening the drive take-up adjustment; remove belt guards as necessary; and then remove the old belt(s). Remove any rust and dirt from take-up rails and lubricate rails if necessary so that tensioning the new belt will be easier. Inspect and repair damaged machine elements (such as worn bearings and bent shafts) to reduce the likelihood of future mechanical trouble and to ensure maximum service from new belts.

V-belts are designed to operate by making clean, dry-surface contact with the sidewall of the sheaves. Inspect belts periodically to assure that they are not contaminated with grease or oil. Don't allow mud, rust or any other foreign matter to build up in sheave grooves. Clean sheaves carefully with a wire brush.

Signs of Trouble
Don't install new V-belts without carefully inspecting the sheaves. Focus special attention on these conditions:

- Worn groove sidewalls,
- A shiny sheave groove bottom,
- Wobbling sheaves or
- Damaged sheaves.

Sheave sidewalls must be perfectly straight because the wedging action of the V-belt is impaired and its gripping power is reduced when the walls are worn or dished out.

A shiny sheave groove bottom is an indication that the belt, sheave or both are badly worn and the belt is bottoming in the

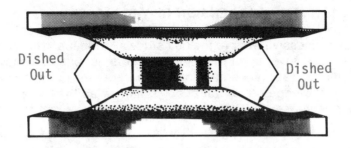

groove. This condition may first be evident on the smaller sheave.

INSTALLING NEW BELTS. Where multiple V-belt drives are used, install all matching belts at the same time. After prolonged operation, V-belts will stretch and if only one belt (of a multiple drive) is new, the new belt will have to carry most of the load. It is more economical to install matched sets of all-new belts from the same manufacturer.

The precaution of storing belts in a cool, dry place will assure maximum V-belt performance when they are finally installed. Deterioration is likely to occur if belts are stored near heat sources or piled on damp floors.

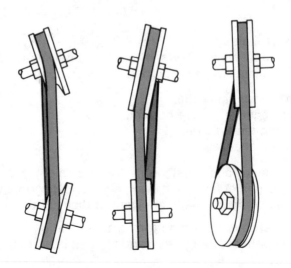

If sheaves are not properly aligned, check to be sure that drive and driven shafts are parallel both horizontally and vertically. The center of drive and driven sheaves should be in a straight line.

Set the belt take-up adjustment at its minimum position and place the new belt in the correct position by hand. Never pry belts over the sheave with a screwdriver or other hard object.

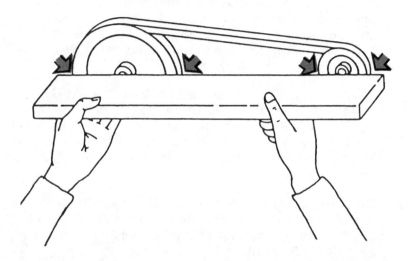

Tighten the drive until slack in the belt is taken up. All V-belt drives must operate with correct belt tension to provide the optimum wedging action of the belt against the groove sidewalls. Refer to the equipment operator's book for tension adjustment procedure.

Allow a reasonable break-in period of a few hours, and then check again for proper belt tension. New belts tend to elongate slightly until they are seated in the sheave groove and initial stretch is removed from the belt.

Be sure to reinstall all protective guards and shields.
Sheave wobble may be caused by:
· improper installation on the shaft,
· a worn/damaged bushing,
· a worn/damaged sheave hub or by
· a bent shaft.

Sheave wobble will cause early failure. The wobbling sheave whips the belt from side to side, subjecting the belt to lateral strain and causing rapid wear to both the sheave and belt. Vibration is another indication of an improperly installed or damaged sheave; however, vibration can also be caused by a damaged belt.

DIESEL FUEL. Diesel fuel lubricates and cools the fuel injection components of the engine in addition to sustaining combustion. Use only CLEAN, HIGH QUALITY fuel of CORRECT GRADE to protect the expensive precision-made components from wear and damage.

The American Society for Testing Materials (ASTM) has adopted certain grade standards to identify different diesel fuels. Each grade of fuel will meet the needs for certain engines in certain operating conditions. Most power equipment manufacturers consider only grades 1-D and 2-D satisfactory for use.

Grade 1-D is more volatile than 2-D. Most manufacturers recommend 1-D for cold temperatures, wide variations in load, frequent speed changes, long periods of idling with low load, and high altitude operation.

Grade 2-D is recommended for warm ambient temperatures, heavy load, high speeds and lower altitudes. The requirements are often conflicting, making selection difficult. Follow the selection guide defined by the manufacturer in the operators manual for the specific equipment.

Cetane Number
Cold starting, warm-up, roughness, acceleration, carbon deposits and exhaust smoke can be affected by the ignition quality of the fuel, which is measured by the cetane method. The minimum cetane number specified by the ASTM for both 1-D and 2-D is 40. The engine manufacturer may suggest fuel with a higher cetane number at low ambient temperature and high altitude. Check with your fuel supplier for availability of fuel with higher cetane ratings.

Contamination

The engine manufacturer often specifies limits of sulfur, water and sediment in the fuel. Usually these are within other regulated limits for fuel sold commercially; however, be sure these limits are not exceeded in the fuel when it is injected into the combustion chamber.

Improper storage and handling can contaminate good fuel. Diesel fuel contains some sulfur and water. Combining the two forms sulfuric acid, which will etch metal parts.

Condensation of moisture in diesel fuel storage tanks occurs more easily than in tanks for gasoline because the more volatile gasoline vapors provide some resistance to the entrance of moisture-laden air. The moisture condenses inside the tank and the water droplets then run into the diesel fuel.

Fill the fuel tanks at the end of each day to reduce air space for condensation. Allow enough time for water and contaminants to settle, and drain water traps at the beginning of each day. Inspect fuel filters often and change them before they become plugged.

Do not store diesel fuel in galvanized containers because the fuel may dissolve the zinc coating, which can then remain in solution until deposited in the pump or injectors. Fuel additives often contain alcohol or another solvent that can dissolve plastic parts. Use additives with extreme caution — only after considering the engine manufacturer's recommendations.

Cloud Point

When the temperature is cold enough, diesel fuel forms wax crystals that will not pass through filters. The temperature at which the crystals form is identified as the *cloud point* because the fuel will appear cloudy. Use fuel with a cloud point at least 10°F (12°C) lower than the lowest anticipated ambient temperature to prevent plugging of the filters in cold weather. Some additives can be safely used to lower the cloud point, but use extreme caution and follow manufacturers' guidelines. Never add alcohol or gasoline to diesel fuel.

Fuel Storage

Diesel fuel should be stored carefully to protect it from contaminants, using large, permanent storage tanks. These permanent storage tanks should be maintained carefully. Fuel from these tanks should be filtered as it is transferred to equipment tanks.

Water requires a long time to settle to the bottom of diesel fuel, necessitating the fuel to stand 12 to 24 hours before the water can be drained.

Observe the following precautions:

☐ Don't ever transfer fuel in an open container.

☐ Don't knock dirt into the tank while filling. Clean the cap before removing it.

☐ Don't store diesel fuel in a galvanized container. The fuel reacts with and dissolves the galvanized coating, later depositing this material in the filters and engine.

☐ Don't store diesel fuel in containers that were previously used for gasoline or other solvent unless the containers are very carefully cleaned. Fine rust and dirt, which will quickly settle out of gasoline, will mix readily with the diesel fuel and cause damage.

☐ Drain the water trap and service filter as suggested by the manufacturer.

☐ If necessary to use smaller containers to transport fuel, make sure the portable containers are clean before filling them with fuel.

GREASE. Throughout the years a complex network of very sophisticated solid and semi-fluid lubricants were developed which are usually called grease. It is very important to recognize that each of these greases is designed for a specific application.

The most important thing to remember about grease is that it is not all alike. Use only the type of grease recommended by the equipment manufacturer.

Grease should do everything that oil does except cool and clean the lubricated parts. Grease should reduce friction, prevent wear and help seal. As with oil, lubrication depends upon the grease being where it is needed, so additives and thickening agents are used to help grease stay in place. As a solid or semi-solid, grease will resist leakage, dripping and throw-off from the lubricated surfaces. Additives are also used to help the grease meet other specific lubrication requirements.

Each type of grease is formulated to meet the needs at different locations and to lubricate under different conditions. Grease should remain stable and in place regardless of the influences of the application. Identification of some popular types are as follows:

Wheel Bearing Grease — Ball or roller wheel bearings require a grease that is able to maintain desired consistency and texture despite temperature, age and mechanical shearing forces. Grease formulated for wheel bearings should also have a high resistance to separation by centrifugal force and provide very good antirust protection.

Universal Joint Grease — Needle roller bearings or plain bushings are used with most universal joints. The limited travel rocking action, high load and sometimes heavy impact imposed upon the universal joint often requires a special type of grease. Manufacturer may suggest a more universally available grease with some applications.

Chassis Grease — The lubricating grease used for most chassis application should provide moderate protection against wear and friction as well as washout protection. Grease is almost always applied with a grease gun through grease fittings. Some manufacturers specify other types of grease for lubricating the chassis especially in high shear or high temperature locations.

ELI (Extended Lubrication Interval) Grease — ELI grease is designed to be installed during manufacture of certain components that do not require relubrication for service life of the part. The design of the part must employ sealed joints to prevent entrance of any water, dirt or other contaminants and to minimize loss of grease. This grease is only seldom available for service, but is listed to show that standard grease is not used if part is not serviced regularly.

Multipurpose Grease — Multipurpose grease is a lubricant of special composition, structure and consistency to meet most performance requirements. Can be substituted for chassis grease, wheel bearing grease, universal joint grease and most other types of grease. The manufacturer of the grease should be consulted if you have specific questions about application. Grease labeled "Multipurpose" indicates that it is different than chassis grease.

Always follow the equipment manufacturer's recommendation when selecting type of grease, service interval and application method. Don't choose grease by price, availability or "Because it looks good." Read the specifications provided by the manufacturer of the grease and compare with recommendations of the equipment manufacturer. If you have questions of either, do not hesitate to question a, or your, dealer or distributor about your application.

Grease is sometimes applied using a grease gun, but disassembly, cleaning and packing by hand is required for many other applications. If a grease fitting (zerk) is used be sure to clean both the fitting and the grease gun connector. Old grease can be purged from some bearings by filling from grease gun until new clean grease is expelled. Seals, boots or neoprene reservoirs may be damaged by attempting to purge grease from bearings that are sealed to prevent grease from leaking out.

LOADING THE VEHICLE

WEIGHT DISTRIBUTION AND LOAD CAPACITY. A properly loaded vehicle will perform better and handle more safely. Store heavier items on or close to the floor and as centrally as possible. Lighter items may be stored in cabinets, closets and drawers. Luggage or similar cargo transported inside your RV should be secured to prevent it from causing damage in case of a sudden stop.

Weight limits recorded on the Federal Certification Sticker or the Vehicle Identification Number plate are maximum limits and exceeding these weights must be considered unsafe. Accurate axle weights are also necessary when determining correct tire inflation pressure. It is therefore extremely important to weigh the vehicle before leaving on a trip.

Vehicle scales are operated at safe ports of entry and other government weight checking stations. These are operated to ensure that vehicles are properly licensed for weight and to make sure that vehicle, axle and hitch weights do exceed safe limits. Private scales are operated at grain elevators, scrap material yards, sand plants, rock quarries and other types of businesses. If your rig exceeds legal weight limits, the benefit of using a private scale is obvious. Always stop and ask permission before pulling onto any scales, unless of course an authorized official orders you onto a scale. You may be charged a nominal fee by the private business and certain times of the day or certain days may be more convenient. Most operators are very helpful, if not busy.

MOTOR HOMES. Located on the dashboard left of the driver position, the driver door latch post, the driver door edge or the drive door hinge pillar is the Federal Certification Sticker. On this sticker is listed the maximum weight carrying capacities of the motor home and each axle.

The Gross Vehicle Weight Rating (GVWR) is the maximum the motor home should weigh with all systems full and with passengers and supplies aboard. Each axle also has a maximum load bearing capacity referred to as the Gross Axle Weight Rating (GAWR).

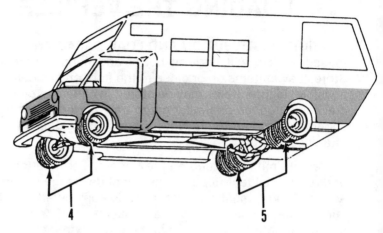

*With only front wheels [4] of motor home on scale, check front axle weight.
With only rear wheels [5] on scale, check rear axle weight.*

With the motor home fully loaded, drive to a scale and weigh the unit as follows: Drive only the front wheels [4] on the scale and obtain the front axle Gross Axle Weight. Next, place the entire vehicle (both axles) on the scale and obtain the Gross Vehicle Weight. Then, drive forward until only the rear wheels [5] are on the scale and obtain the rear axle Gross Axle Weight. Compare the Gross Vehicle Weight with the GVWR on the Federal Sticker. If the Gross Vehicle Weight exceeds the GVWR, it will be necessary to reduce total vehicle load. If the Gross Vehicle Weight is less than the GVWR, check front and rear axle Gross Axle Weights against the front and rear GAWR on the Federal Sticker. If either axle weight exceeds the GAWR for that axle, redistribute enough equipment to ensure that loads on front and rear axles are within the required limit.

The following may be helpful for recording limits from the Federal Certification Sticker and the actual weights when motorhome is fully loaded.

Federal Certification Sticker

[1] GAWR (Front Axle) _____ pounds
[2] (Rear Axle) . . . . _____ pounds
[3] GVWR . . . . _____ pounds

Actual Weights and Tire Pressure

[4] (Front Axle) _____ lbs. _____ psi
[5] (Rear Axle) _____ lbs. _____ psi
[6] Total Weight _____ lbs.

Actual loaded weights of axles should be compared to the rated limits listed on the Federal Certification Sticker. Actual weight listed on lines 4, 5 and 6 should be less than limits from sticker recorded on lines 1, 2 and 3. It may be necessary to move or remove items to change distribution of weight or to reduce weight. Improper loading may affect handling and cause motorhome to be difficult to control.

CAMPING TRAILERS AND TRAVEL TRAILERS. Federal Certification Sticker is located on the left exterior wall of the trailer, near the front. The sticker gives the maximum weight carrying capacity of the trailer and each axle.

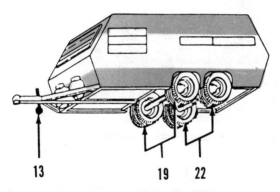

View showing weighing points of tandem axle travel trailer. Refer to text.

The Gross Vehicle Weight Rating (GVWR) is the maximum the trailer should weigh with water and LP-Gas tanks full and with food, clothing and all other supplies aboard. Each axle also has a maximum load bearing capacity referred to as the Gross Axle Weight Rating (GAWR).

When loading the trailer, store heavy gear first, keeping it on or as close to floor as possible. Heavy items should be stored

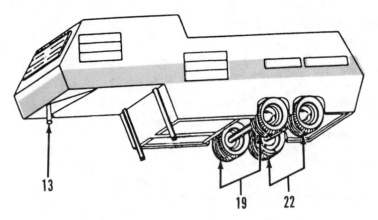

Weighing points of a typical fifth wheel trailer.

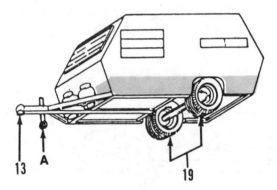

Weighing points of a single axle travel trailer.

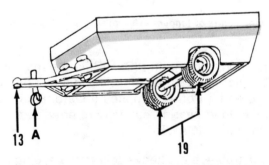

Weighing points of a fold-down camping trailer.

directly over or slightly ahead of the axle(s). Store only light items on high shelves. Distribute weight to obtain even side-to-side balance of the loaded vehicle.

Approximate hitch weight of lightweight trailers can be measured by locating the scales under the tongue support jack (A). Although not exactly the same as exerted against the hitch ball, this weight measurement is reasonably close.

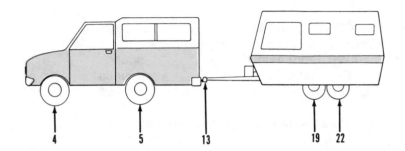

Hitch weight of most trailers is measured by weighing the tow vehicle while the trailer is attached, then weighing the tow vehicle without the trailer. The difference in the weights is the hitch weight. Be sure that the same number of occupants, etc., are in the tow vehicles during both measurements.

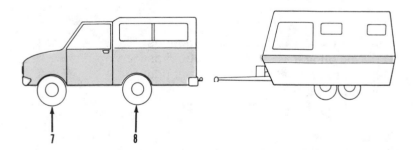

Be sure that actual hitch weight does not exceed the limits of the trailer hitch. Also be sure that axle weight limits of the tow vehicle are not exceeded.

Actual weighing can be easily accomplished by weighing each axle of the towing vehicle and the trailer separately. Disconnect the trailer, then weigh each axle of the similarly loaded tow vehicle. Passengers and other cargo should remain in tow vehicle during both weight checks.

The following may be helpful for determining hitch weights, comparing actual weights with limits posted on the Federal Certification Stickers and for recording recommended tire pressures.

TOW VEHICLE DATA
Federal Certification Sticker
[1] GAWR (Front Axle) _____pounds
[2]   (Rear Axle) . . . . . _____pounds
(3) GVWR . . . . _____pounds

With Trailer, Actual Weight and Tire Pressure
[4] Front Axle . . . . _____ lbs. _____ psi
[5] Rear Axle . . . . _____ lbs. _____ psi
[6] Total Weight . . _____ lbs.

Without Trailer, Actual Weight and Tire Pressure
[7] Front Axle . . . . _____ lbs. _____ psi
[8] Rear Axle . . . . _____ lbs. _____ psi
[9] Total Weight . . _____ lbs.

HITCH
[10] Limit . . . . _____ pounds
[11] Copy line 6 . . . . . _____ pounds
[12] Subtract line 9 . . _____ pounds
[13] Actual Hitch
        Weight . . . . _____ pounds

TRAILER
Federal Certification Sticker
[14] GAWR (Front
          Axle) . . . . _____ pounds
[15]   _____ pounds
[16]   _____ pounds
[17] (Rear Axle) . . . . . . _____ pounds
[18] GVWR . . . . _____ pounds

Actual Weights and Tire Pressure

[19] Front Axle... _____ lbs. _____ psi
[20]   _____ lbs. _____ psi
[21]   _____ lbs. _____ psi
[22] Rear Axle ... _____ lbs. _____ psi
[23] Copy line 13 . _____ lbs.
[24] Total .... _____ lbs.

Actual loaded weights of axles should be compared to the rated limits listed on the Federal Certification Stickers. For the tow vehicle, weights listed on lines, 4, 5 and 6 should be less than limits from sticker on lines 1, 2 and 3. Actual hitch weight on line 13 should not be more than limit recorded on line 10. Trailer weight limits recorded on lines 14 through 18 should be compared to similar lines 19, 20, 21, 22 and 24 which lists actual weights.

It may be necessary to move or remove items to change the distribution of weight or to reduce weight. Changes, especially major ones, are not easily accomplished on a trip, while broken down or to comply with a law that you have violated.

TRUCK CAMPERS. Standard sizes of pick-up truck cargo beds permit an owner to install a very heavy camper on a truck designed for only light duty. The combination may result in damage, poor performance, hazardous handling and possible injury. The Federal Certification Sticker is provided to inform you of limits that are considered safe. Exceeding the limits almost ensures poor performance, dangerous handling and extensive damage. Select a truck that has a Gross Vehicle Weight Rating (GVWR) higher than the total weight of the truck, camper, cargo and hitch weight (if you are pulling a trailer). Also be careful not to exceed the Gross Axle Weight Rating (GAWR) for either axle.

When loading the camper, store heavy gear first, keeping it on or as close to the floor as possible. Place heavy things far enough forward to keep the loaded campers center of gravity within the zone recommended by the truck manufacturer. Store only light objects on high shelves. Distribute weight to obtain even side-to-side balance of the loaded vehicle.

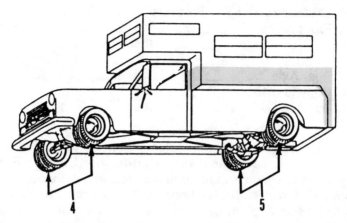

With only front wheels [4] of truck camper on scale, check front axle weight. With only rear wheels [5] on scale, check rear axle weight. Refer to text.

When truck and camper are loaded, drive to a scale and weigh the front axle [4] and rear [5] separately to determine axle loads.

The following may be helpful for recording limits from the Federal Certification Sticker, actual weights and recommended tire pressures.

Federal Certification Sticker
[1] GAWR (Front Axle) . . . . _____ pounds
[2] (Rear Axle) . . . . _____ pounds
[3] GVWR . . . . _____ pounds

Actual Weights and Tire Pressure
[4] Front Axle _____ lbs. _____ psi
[5] Rear Axle _____ lbs. _____ psi
[6] Total Weight _____ lbs.
Tire pressure without camper should be:
    Front _____ psi
    Rear _____ psi

If the actual weight [lines 4, 5 and 6] exceeds the limit listed in similar lines 1, 2 and 3, move or remove items to bring all weights below the ratings.

TOW VEHICLE

OPTIONAL EQUIPMENT. If you plan to tow your trailer with the vehicle you now own, consult your automobile or truck dealership for help in determining tow weight capabilities.

If you are buying a new vehicle to tow your trailer, you should follow the recommendations of the auto manufacturer in making your selection. All the major auto manufacturers have studied the special needs of their vehicles for towing use and have printed brochures to help you properly match the tow vehicle equipment to your particular sized trailer.

Among optional items which may be important for optimum performance are:

a. Axle ratio
b. Increased engine cooling system
c. Transmission cooler
d. Alternator and battery size
e. Suspension system
f. Tire size or rating

Depending on the weight of your trailer and the type of driving you are planning, the auto manufacturer may or may not recommend all of the available options. Generally most of the towing options are recommended for extensive traveling under any conditions, mountain driving, hot climate driving or when towing heavy class trailers.

Even with all the options, try to avoid any type driving that will overheat your engine such as following a slow-moving truck up a long grade.

HITCHES

Hitches commonly used to pull camping and travel trailers are divided into four classes.

Class I — can be used for trailers with gross weight less than 2000 lbs. and tongue weight 10-15% of the Gross Trailer Weight. This hitch class may be either weight carrying or weight distributing (equalizing) type.

Class II — can be used for trailers with gross weight of 2001 through 3500 lbs. and tongue weight 10-15% of the Gross Trailer Weight. This hitch class may be either weight carrying or weight distributing (equalizing) type.

Class III — can be used for trailers with gross weight of 3501 through 5000 lbs. and tongue weight 15% of the Gross Trailer Weight. This hitch class must be of the weight distributing (equalizing) type.

Class IV — can be used for trailers with gross weight of more than 5000 lbs. and tongue weight should be 15% of the Gross Trailer Weight. This hitch class must be of the weight distributing (equalizing) type and must have anti-sway device.

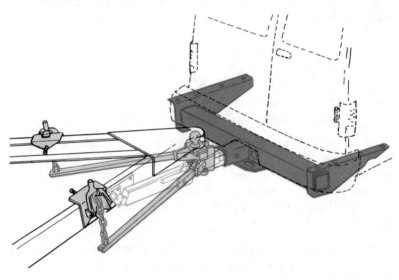

Weight carrying hitches are often attached to or are part of the tow vehicle's rear bumper; however, they may be attached to the frame or body of the tow vehicle. Most weight carrying hitches are marked with tongue weight limits which are considered by the manufacturer to be the maximum safe limit when properly installed. Never exceed this marked limit and, if not marked, never exceed 300 lbs. tongue weight for any weight carrying hitch. Weight carrying hitches should not be attached to any shock absorbing bumpers.

Weight distributing or "equalizer hitches" should be installed on the tow vehicle only by qualified personnel. The frame, that is attached to the tow vehicle's frame or body is often called the "receiver" or "hitch receiver". It is important to attach this hitch receiver correctly to the tow vehicle by welding or bolting solidly to the vehicle frame or body. The hitch ball is attached to a hitch bar which is installed in the hitch receiver. The height and angle of the hitch ball should be the correct position as determined by the tow vehicle and the trailer. Adjustment of the hitch ball height and angle should be carefully accomplished by your RV dealer. Satisfaction with trailers is determined to a large extent by the proper selection, installation and adjustment of the hitch assembly.

Fifth wheel trailers are towed by vehicles which use special hitches usually mounted in the bed of a pick-up truck. Several variations are available and the dealer will help with both selection and installation.

EQUALIZER HITCHES. In addition to pulling the weight of a trailer, a tow vehicle must also support about 10% to 15% of the actual weight of the trailer at the hitch point. With a 6000 pound trailer, this additional weight might be 900 pounds. This much weight added to the rear of the tow vehicle can alter balance and will probably result in poor steering control, poor braking control and can be potentially dangerous. Use of heavier springs, spring helpers or stiffer tires will not correct the basic out-of-balance condition. The problems from this condition are compounded when traveling over bumps and dips in the road. The balance problem is solved by addition of a suitably matched "equalizer hitch". The effect of an equalizer hitch is to distribute the hitch load equally between the front and rear tow vehicle axles and the trailer axle(s). Instead of the entire hitch weight sitting on the car's rear bumper, it is evenly distributed to the three axle areas and your tow vehicle can remain relatively level. This will not only give you better steering and brake control, but will keep your headlight beams down on the road where they belong.

Most hitch manufacturers offer equalizing hitches designed to handle trailers of various hitch weight classes. Your dealer will help you select the right size hitch required for your trailer weight.

SWAY CONTROLS. Except for the very light camping trailers and small travel trailers, most trailers should employ some type of sway control device. There are several types of these devices available operating on different principles such as friction, cam action and computer operated braking of the trailer wheels. Each has some advantages over the others as their manufacturers literature will tell you. They will all decrease the sway effects induced by passing trucks and busses or strong side winds. They can make towing safer when driving under adverse conditions.

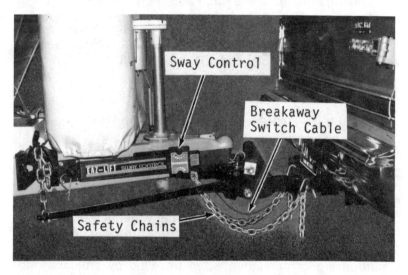

SAFETY CHAINS. There are different safety chain requirements by the various states. As delivered, your vehicle was equipped to meet the state requirements where purchased. Heavier and/or additional chains with case hardened quick connect links may be desired. Always have the safety chains attached when towing. Install them in a manner so they do not restrict sharp turns of the tow vehicle-trailer combination, but tight enough so they do not drag on the road.

BREAKAWAY SWITCH. The breakaway switch uses either a large dry cell or the auxiliary 12 volt battery contained within the trailer to automatically engage the trailer brakes if the trailer is accidentally detached from the tow vehicle. A cable is used to attach an engagement pin to the tow vehicle. The pin is inserted in the breakaway switch to hold the switch open. If the trailer is detached, the cable will pull the pin from the switch and the breakaway switch will then apply electrical current to the trailer brakes.

Occasionally, pull the pin out and check the braking action. It is difficult to tell the condition of dry cell batteries. Storage batteries, kept well charged, are recommended for this emergency braking circuit.

HITCHING. Before starting the hitching operation, remove the jacks from beneath the trailer by raising and lowering the trailer hitch jack. As soon as the coupler is lowered over the hitch ball, fasten the latching mechanism and fasten the safety pin or other safety device provided. Attach the spring bars with chains or other hitch devices provided, attach the electric connecting plug and position the pin in the breakaway switch. Crank trailer hitch jack to its highest position and remove chocks from in front and behind the trailer wheels. Before starting down the road, check trailer running lights, stop lights, turn signal lights and brake operation.

UNHITCHING. The site for parking your trailer should be as level as possible so less jacking will be required to level the trailer. The ground should also be firm enough that the jacks will not sink.

Before unhitching, place chocks in front and behind the wheels on both sides of trailer. Remove the safety chains and the breakaway switch pin and the trailer electrical plug from their receptacles. Place a block under the hitch jack and extend jack to meet it firmly. Remove the equalizer hitch spring bars in accordance with the hitch manufacturers instructions. The safety latch on the hitch coupler should now be released and the hitch jacked up until it clears the hitch ball. You can now remove the tow vehicle and proceed to level the trailer.

TRAILER TOWING

ON HIGHWAY. Assuming your tow vehicle is reasonably adequate for the trailer to be pulled and that your hitch is suitable, towing is not much more difficult than driving the family car by itself unless adverse weather or traffic conditions are encountered.

Before traveling down the highway, double check your hitch to see that all is in order, safety pins engaged, breakaway cable connected, safety chains attached and that lights and brakes are operating normally. Adjust mirrors for best coverage, being careful to stay within legal width limit. Your mirrors should extend out far enough to see down both sides and slightly behind the trailer.

If you are going to be driving through any large cities via multiple lane highways, check out the route in advance. Use metropolitan area maps to determine the lanes you should be in at critical points. Remember that now you have another vehicle in tow and you cannot "jump" lanes at the last moment.

Never change lanes without first turning on indicators, looking to ensure that you are going to be clear and then cautiously proceed. If you miss a freeway exit because you are in the wrong lane, just miss it and get off at the next convenient one. If you continually "challenge" traffic and take chances in order to get the right of way, sooner or later it may needlessly involve you and your family in a serious accident. Plan ahead, take it easy and be courteous.

When driving over two-lane roads, take special care in passing. Remember that your car-trailer combination cannot accelerate as fast as the car alone. Be sure you have plenty of clear space for passing and don't return to the right hand lane until you are sure your trailer clears the passed vehicle. Truck drivers often flash their headlights to indicate clearance for safe return to the right hand lane. Many trailerists return the favor.

Drive sensibly when it comes to speed. You may need more space to safely stop a trailer and tow vehicle combination than your car or truck by itself. Trailer brakes should be adjusted to engage before the tow vehicle brakes. Be especially cautious about applying brakes heavily when the tow vehicle and trailer are not in a straight line. Slow down on wet surfaces.

When turning with trailer attached, the trailer will "cut inside" of the tow vehicle track. Remember to allow for this when making sharp turns around obstacles such as curbs, trees and gas pumps.

Make full use of a convex mirror at least on the right side. This will give you vision where the flat mirror may not. Be especially cautious until you become accustomed to the perspective the convex mirror displays. Vehicles appear to be a greater distance behind you than they really are, when viewed in the convex mirror surface.

If your model trailer is a "wide-track", take extra care when towing on narrow roads. Your car wheels could be well on the concrete while the trailer wheels are off and on the shoulder. In some areas, shoulders are extremely soft after heavy rains and you must make every effort to keep the trailer on the hard road surface. If the road has a sharp edge with a drop of several inches to the soft shoulder, don't try to bring the trailer back onto hard surface of road until reducing vehicle speed. If a trailer is sharply returned at high speed, sometimes it will "catch" the concrete edge suddenly and swerve dangerously towards the other side of the highway before finally straightening out.

Avoid driving on ice covered highways. Driving on packed dry snow is not advisable, but you can be reasonably safe under these conditions if you are used to them and use caution. Sometimes a highway is ice free but overpasses and bridges are frozen over. When crossing iced bridges, maintain constant speed in a straight line to avoid skidding.

OFF HIGHWAY. When traveling off the hard surface road, remember that gravel, sand or dirt offer less traction to your wheels in both accelerating and stopping situations and especially in hill climbing. If you must take your trailer to the bottom of a steep hill, be sure the return route up to the top of the hill is straight enough that you can make a run for it. Loosening your equalizer bar chains or adding rocks or other weights to your car trunk might get you out of a tight spot if you stall, slipping your drive wheels on a very steep hill. If not, you may have to call for help from another tow vehicle. Roads causing this kind of problem are rare but some of the most beautiful campgrounds might have just such an entrance.

A good rule to follow on deciding whether to go "down into" a camp area from a major road, is to stop at the main road and walk down first. Observe the size of trailers already parked and what type tow vehicles brought them in. If yours is comparable, it's reasonable to assume you can get in and out also. Take a good look at where you can park and plan your approach to maneuver for parking. Take into consideration any sharp turns, low branches, large boulders on roads edge or any other obstacles which could cause damage. If you have a heavy trailer and all you see in camp are lightweights, check carefully to make sure that your larger rig can enter safely, park comfortably and leave easily. Steep loose graveled grades are much easier to drive down than to pull a heavy load up. Camping will be more enjoyable for all in your party if you are careful not to get your RV into a situation that requires help (sometimes professional help) to get out.

Some RVs have more ground clearance than others. If your model has an extra low holding tank and/or plumbing traps, etc., take that into consideration when traveling unsurfaced roads. Roads with a high center crown containing boulders can damage under chassis plumbing.

Long trailers and trailers which have very little ground clearance may drag on the ground when coming out of a dip. Skid bars will help in many situations, but usually will not protect from damage caused by high center as well as a dip.

Tight turns, even on paved roads, should be examined carefully if you are towing a trailer which is extra long. The tow vehicle may be able to follow the road only if the trailer cuts across the corner. Trees, curbs, boulders, soft shoulders, etc., may damage the trailer if pulled across the inside of the turn. The rear of the trailer may also swing in an arc that is also occupied by a tree, building, post, etc.

Be careful of overhead obstacles which could damage the top of the trailer or roof mounted accessories. It is a good idea to measure the height of tallest part of your rig before traveling, then record this measurement inside the tow vehicle so that you will know the necessary clearance. Even small limbs can cause a great amount of damage. Antennas, windows and vents are especially easily damaged particularly at highway speed or when extended (opened).

Trees that lean in towards the roadway at an angle can be deceiving and it it easy to misjudge clearance and badly scrape a top edge. A good way to pass by obstacles is to position observers where they can guide you by safely.

If you intend to do much off highway travel, carry along an axe, small bucksaw, a shovel and a couple of three or four foot boards that can be used to aid you in getting unstuck. Also carry along a tow chain or cable. A power winch may also be a practical option.

Loosen tension of sway bars when maneuvering in and out of camp areas to reduce stiffness in turning. In slick conditions of snow and ice, loosen sway bar adjustments. In extreme cases, overtightened sway bars could force your tow vehicle to go straight ahead instead of turning in the direction you turn it.

DRIVING MOTOR HOME
OR TRUCK CAMPER

ON HIGHWAY. Driving your motor home or truck camper is comparable to driving your family car once you become accustomed to the feel of the controls and to the reference points from the drivers seat relating to the position of the RV in traffic. Be cautious when maneuvering to allow for the length, width and height of the vehicle. Always allow extra room in cornering and when changing lanes. Check the side mirrors often. Learn to use the view of the roadway behind, as seen through the side mirrors, as a reference to keep a good lane position.

Avoid sudden maneuvers when passing another vehicle. Remember that additional time and distance are required to pass safely. Wait until the road is clear of oncoming traffic for at least ½-mile. Check the rearview mirrors and signal lane change before passing. When you are safely ahead of the other vehicle, signal lane change and return to your original lane.

Drive with consideration on the highway, observing all applicable speed and safety regulations. The best cruising speed for your RV will vary with road and weather conditions. Remember that higher speeds may result in a sharp increase in fuel consumption.

Allow a safe distance in which to stop your RV. Never follow another vehicle closer than one vehicle length for each 10 mph. Pump the brake pedal lightly to stop on wet or icy roads. If you start to slide, turn steering wheel in the direction of the slide. DO NOT tromp the brake pedal as a panic stop will increase the slide. Do not rest your foot on the brake pedal when you are not intending to stop. "Riding" the brakes will waste fuel and can cause excessive brake temperatures, lining wear and possible brake failure.

Driving on winding or mountain roads is not difficult if done with reasonable care. Observe proper vehicle speeds when ascending or descending hills and always operate in the proper transmission range. Downshift on hills to avoid overheating or undue engine loads.

Allow for the extra height of your RV and avoid areas having low overhead clearance. It is a good idea to measure the height of the tallest part of your rig before traveling, then record this measurement within sight of the driver so that you will quickly know the necessary clearance. Obstacles are often marked with actual vertical clearance and some that appear very high are not enough for a tall vehicle. Be especially careful of low hanging tree branches or other obstructions whenever you drive or park. Avoid low roofs when pulling in for service. This may be particularly important if you drive with the overhead vents open or if the RV is equipped with a roof air conditioner.

If you are pulling a trailer or another vehicle behind your motorhome or truck camper, be especially careful and always know the condition and position of the vehicle that is being towed. A lightweight boat, car or trailer is hardly noticeable to the driver of a motorhome used as a tow vehicle, but don't change lanes too quickly. Remember the additional length. Also notice regularly the position of the vehicle or trailer that you are towing. An abrupt change in the position of the towed vehicle or trailer may indicate a flat tire, a brake or axle bearing that is locked up or some other problem. A flat tire on the lightweight trailer may not be noticeable to driver of the towing vehicle until something very dramatic happens like the boat falling off. Drivers following or passing you pointing toward the rear may be cause for concern.

OFF HIGHWAY. Some campgrounds do not accept reservations, but make one whenever you can. If possible, arrive early so you may inspect and choose a site during daylight hours. Try to avoid sites near a swamp, stream or other bodies of water that may harbor mosquitoes or other insects. Avoid parking under dead trees or loose limbs which might fall and cause injury or damage. Stay away from areas which show signs of flash flooding. DO NOT park on private property without first obtaining permission.

When driving through camp areas, be aware of overhead obstacles which could cause extensive damage to roof mounted RV antennas, roof vents or roof mounted air conditioners. Trees that lean in towards the roadway at an angle can be deceiving and it is easy to misjudge clearance and badly scrape a top edge. A good way to pass by obstacles is to position an observer where they can guide you by safely.

If you intend to do much off highway travel, carry along an axe, small bucksaw, a shovel and a couple of three or four foot boards that can be used to aid you in getting unstuck. A tow chain or cable are sometimes helpful and a power winch may be a practical option.

⚠CAUTION

If stuck, do not race the engine or spin the wheels. Prolonged efforts to free a stuck vehicle may result in damage to engine, transmission or rear axle.

LEVELING AND STABILIZATION

GENERAL. Most RVs require leveling and stabilizing (blocking up) with some kind of jacks for comfortable occupancy. But, more important, the unit must be level in order for the absorption type gas refrigerator and drainage system, both which function by gravity, to operate properly. Place a level on the bottom of the refrigerator freezer compartment or in a normally level location inside the vehicle to determine proper levelness. Bubble levels are furnished with some refrigerators and are available at your RV dealers. Use leveling blocks under wheels to obtain side-to-side levelness. After leveling, check that wheel chocks are tight against tires.

When the unit has been leveled side-to-side and front-to-back, you may wish to permanently attach levels on the front and/or back and sides of the trailer or truck camper or inside near the driver, on the sidewall and dash panel of a motor home. This will allow you to tell at a glance if you have stopped on a level site, and will help speed up the leveling process.

Various types of screw type stabilizer jack stands are available to block the RV in a level position. Some are free standing type while others are permanently installed on bottom of the RV.

MISCELLANEOUS

HOT WEATHER OPERATION. When possible, always select a parking site where your RV will be shaded during the hottest part of the day. Awnings over each window, or especially those covering the full length of the RV, are especially helpful in keeping the inside temperature down.

Roof mounted air conditioners are very desirable for very hot climates. One precaution should be kept in mind for their operation, however. For proper operation of any motor, especially those in an air conditioner, it is important that the line voltage not be too low. Low voltage causes motors to run hotter than they should and their life is therefore shortened. The line voltage in many campgrounds is unfortunately not as high as it should be, especially when there is a heavy load on it such as many other air conditioners. The use of an extension cord to supply power to your RV should be avoided for it often causes a drop in your available voltage. Dim lights and narrowing of your TV picture are indicators of low voltage. It is a good idea to check available voltage with a voltmeter. Air conditioners are designed to operate properly between 110 and 120 volts. Running them at lower voltages will shorten their life.

COLD WEATHER OPERATION. The most important precaution in cold weather operation is:

Cooking appliances need fresh air for safe operation. Before operation:
1. Open overhead vent or turn on exhaust fan, and
2. Open window.

A warning label has been located in the cooking area to remind you to provide an adequate supply of fresh air for combustion. Unlike homes, the amount of oxygen supply is limited due to the size of the recreational vehicle, and proper ventilation when using the cooking appliance(s) will avoid dangers of asphyxiation. It is especially important that cooking appliances not be used for comfort heating as the danger of asphyxiation is greater when the appliance is used for long periods of time.

The furnace, water heater and gas refrigerator are all designed to seal the combustion area from the inside of the RV. This is for your safety to prevent asphyxiation from carbon monoxide or depletion of oxygen. If your furnace does not have sufficient capacity to heat your RV comfortably in the climate where you are using it, you should replace it with a larger capacity furnace. The use of the range or oven to provide supplementary heat is very dangerous and often fatal.

If you find frost or condensation in the closets or cabinets during long periods of cold weather operation, leave the doors to these areas standing open a little to provide air circulation to dispel the moisture.

CAMPGROUND COURTESY. The "golden rule" should never be forgotten in the campground. Treat other campers as you want to be treated. The most common complaints are noise (radios, exhaust, voices, etc.), children (with or without vehicles) and dogs (barking, frightening, odor, etc.). If you are not a considerate camper, others may assume that you want to be treated similarly and be very offensive to you.

Common courtesy will help make your stay more pleasant. Being considerate of your neighbors will help make friends. Campsites are often close together and loud noises may disturb your neighbors. Follow the posted rules of the campsite. Open fires may not be permitted. If you can build a campfire, clear the area of flammable materials. Never leave a campfire unattended and always make certain the embers are completely extinguished before leaving the site. Put all litter in proper receptacles and leave your site neat and clean. Don't let your water or sewer line leak. Drive slowly through camp areas at any hour for the safety of pedestrians and to prevent making a lot of dust.

VISITING CANADA OR MEXICO. Passports or visas are not required for entry into Canada or Mexico. However, tourist cards are necessary for Mexico if you will be staying more than 72 hours or travel farther than 40 miles from the border. Cards can be obtained at the port of entry or from a Mexican consulate. You should carry your birth certificate, voters registration card, baptismal certificate or similar proof of identity when entering either country. Naturalized U.S. citizens should carry their naturalization papers or other proof of citizenship. Persons under 18 years of age should carry a notarized letter from their parents or guardians giving them permission to travel in Canada or Mexico.

No special drivers license or permit is necessary in either country, but renew your license if it will expire during the trip. Proof of vehicle ownership is required at the border. If you are using someone else's unit, you should have a notarized letter authorizing its use. Mexico requires a vehicle permit for every self-propelled vehicle. The permit can only be obtained from Mexican customs offices upon presentation of a tourist card, vehicle registration and title or notarized statement from owner.

CB radio operation in Canada requires a temporary license which can be obtained by writing Regional Director, Telecommunications Regulation Branch, Department of Communications, 20th Floor, 2085 Union Avenue, Montreal, Quebec H3A 2C3, Canada. Mexico currently prohibits the use of CB radios.

In Canada, each province has its own hunting and fishing laws and license requirements. You must provide a written description and the serial number of each gun at the border. Hand guns and fully automatic firearms are prohibited in Canada. A license must be obtained from the province in which you intend to fish or hunt. Further information can be obtained by writing Department of Lands and Forests, Wildlife Branch, in the province you intend to visit. Hunting and fishing laws in Mexico are extremely complicated. Request further information from Secretaria de Communicaciones, Estados Unidos Mexicanos, Mexico DF.

SUPPLIES AND EQUIPMENT

SUPPLIES. Following is a list that may be helpful for selecting supplies and equipment considered necessities for traveling in the RV:

Personal Items
- ☐ Tooth brushes & tooth paste
- ☐ Hair brushes, combs & hair drier
- ☐ Bath soap, shampoo & deodorant
- ☐ Wash cloths & towels
- ☐ Shaving equipment & makeup
- ☐ Bedding, pillow, blankets (electric?) & sleeping bags
- ☐ Rain gear
- ☐ Clothes
- ☐ Glasses (sight or sun) & Care kit for contacts
- ☐ Sun protection lotion & sunburn cream
- ☐ Medication
- ☐ _____
- ☐ _____
- ☐ _____
- ☐ _____

Cooking Utensils
- ☐ Coffe/tea pot
- ☐ Skillet, pans (with lids) and griddle
- ☐ Sharp knives (carving, paring & steak)
- ☐ Chopping board
- ☐ Cooking fork, spatula & tongs
- ☐ Spoons (serving & measuring)
- ☐ Hot pads
- ☐ Bowls (mixing, serving, cereal & soup)
- ☐ Openers (can, bottle, corkscrew)
- ☐ Appliances (mixer, toaster)
- ☐ Portable barbeque grille, charcoal, lighter fluid & cooking utensils
- ☐ _____
- ☐ _____
- ☐ _____
- ☐ _____

Food Serving Supplies

- ☐ Plates, bowls, glasses, cups & saucers (washable or disposable)
- ☐ Flatware (knives, forks & spoons)
- ☐ Salt, Pepper & other condiments
- ☐ Napkins, table cloths & place mats
- ☐ _____
- ☐ _____
- ☐ _____
- ☐ _____

Cleaning Supplies and Equipment

- ☐ Waste basket & litter bags
- ☐ Broom, dust pan, mop & portable vacuum cleaner
- ☐ Laundry bag, soap, clothes line & clothes pins
- ☐ Room deodorizer (air freshener)
- ☐ Dish pans, soap & cleanser
- ☐ Dish cloths, scouring pads, sponges & towels
- ☐ Toilet bowl cleaning brush, etc.
- ☐ _____
- ☐ _____
- ☐ _____
- ☐ _____

Miscellaneous Supplies & Support Equipment

- ☐ Alarm clock & radio
- ☐ Facial & toilet tissue (bio-degradable)
- ☐ Chemical for toilet
- ☐ Water filter supplies
- ☐ Scissors & sewing kit
- ☐ Paper towels, aluminum foil, wax paper & plastic wrap
- ☐ Plastic bags (sandwich, garbage, etc.)
- ☐ Folding chairs
- ☐ Camera & supplies
- ☐ Binoculars
- ☐ Games, cards, books & magazines
- ☐ Sewer hose extension
- ☐ High pressure water hose, "Y" connectors & adapters
- ☐ Heavy duty extension cords & adapters
- ☐ Sporting (fishing, skiiing, etc.) equipment
- ☐ Leveling blocks & small carpenter's level

Miscellaneous Supplies & Support Equipment Cont.

- ☐ Wheel chocks
- ☐ Insect repellent
- ☐ Portable fan
- ☐ Night light
- ☐ _____
- ☐ _____
- ☐ _____
- ☐ _____

Emergency Equipment
- ☐ Flashlight & lantern (Fresh batteries, fluid & mantel)
- ☐ Matches
- ☐ First Aid Kit
  - ☐ Adhesive bandages (assorted sizes)
  - ☐ Adhesive tape
  - ☐ Antacid
  - ☐ Anti-bacterial ointment, spray, liquid
  - ☐ Antiseptic soap
  - ☐ Aspirin or equivalent
  - ☐ Bandages (assorted size gauze pads)
  - ☐ Burn cream & sunburn medicine
  - ☐ Elastic bandages
  - ☐ Eye wash
  - ☐ Hot water bottle
  - ☐ Motion sickness medicine
  - ☐ Snake bite kit
  - ☐ Thermometer
  - ☐ _____
  - ☐ _____

- ☐ Saw, hatchet, axe & shovel
- ☐ Assortment of hand tools & lug wrench
- ☐ Small jack & boards for blocking
- ☐ Spare wheel & tire (check air pressure before leaving)
- ☐ Tire pump & tire pressure gage
- ☐ Fire extinguisher(s), road flares & reflectors
- ☐ Tow chain or cable & jumper cables
- ☐ Spare fuses & light bulbs

Emergency Equipment Cont.

☐ Extra oil (engine, transmission, outboard motor, etc.)
☐ _____
☐ _____
☐ _____
☐ _____

HELPFUL HINTS

The following notes and hints are provided by readers of the earlier edition of this book, industry personnel and our staff. We want you to have safe, fun trips and hope these suggestions are helpful. You may also contribute to subsequent editions by writing to:

RV Editorial Director
INTERTEC Publishing Corporation
P.O. Box 12901
Overland Park, KS 66282-2901

Gather information about where you will be going from all available sources before leaving. Suggested places to look for information are:

Auto clubs   Libraries (public & private)
Book stores   R.V. clubs
Chamber of Commerce   Travel publications

Also, don't overlook the wealth of information available from friends. Often spectacular but little known points of interest are discovered by talking to people who have "been there" or "lived near there awhile."

Make as **many** reservations as possible and as **early** as possible. Good places often fill up early. Rescheduling is easier if you know well in advance.

Plan your route and always keep someone informed of where you are and will be. Your safety or the safety of others could be determined by how quickly you can be reached or found. Interstate highways are faster and more direct, but are seldom as enjoyable, scenic or interesting as less traveled routes. Be sure to keep daily travel distances realistic don't try to go too far in too short a time.

Avoid carrying large amounts of money. Use traveler's checks and a small number of credit cards. If lost or stolen, one credit card is trouble enough. Don't multiply the difficulty more by carrying too many cards. Budget carefully and plan expenses as completely as possible before leaving. Don't make the trip a financial disaster.

Become familiar with your insurance policies. Check with your agent before leaving to be sure that you have proper forms, telephone numbers and coverage.